How Well Does Your Child Read?

A Step-by-Step Assessment of Your Child's Reading Skills and Techniques to Improve Them

By

Ann Cook

Illustrated by

Holly Forsyth

CAREER PRESS
3 Tice Road
P.O. Box 687
Franklin Lakes, NJ 07417
1-800-CAREER-1
201-848-0310 (NJ and outside U.S.)
FAX: 201-848-1727

Copyright © 1997 by Ann Cook

HOW WELL DOES YOUR CHILD READ?
ISBN 1-56414-303-1, $9.99
Cover design by Robert Howard
Printed in the U.S.A. by Book-mart Press

To order this title by mail, please include price as noted above, $2.50 handling per order, and $1.50 for each book ordered. Send to: Career Press, Inc., 3 Tice Road, P.O. Box 687, Franklin Lakes, NJ 07417.

Or call toll-free 1-800-CAREER-1 (in NJ and Canada: 201-848-0310) to order using VISA or MasterCard, or for further information on books from Career Press.

Library of Congress Cataloging-in-Publication Data

Cook, Ann, 1954-
    How well does your child read? : a step-by-step assessment of your
child's reading skills and techniques to improve them / by Ann Cook.
        p. cm.
    Includes index.
    ISBN 1-56414-303-1 (pbk.)
    1. Reading (Elementary) -- Ability testing -- United States.
    2. Reading -- Phonetic method -- United States.   I. Title.
LB1573.C55626   1997
372.48--dc21   97-13343
                                                                         CIP

For Nate

Special thanks to Kim Ebner, Pat Weideman,
Christie Savage, and Joan Di Giacomo.

For referral to a qualified testing or
tutoring center, call 800-457-4255 or e-mail
testingkids@earthlink.net

Contents

Introduction

You've probably noticed that times have changed since you were in school. The work your child brings home seems quite different from what you were learning at that age. Children today are expected to know more and possess more advanced skills at an earlier age. You're left to wonder: "What is normal for a child in my child's grade?" or "What are the national standards in reading?"

You also begin to worry that report cards and scores on standardized tests aren't telling you enough about how your child is *really* performing academically. After all, news reports are assaulting you with discouraging statistics about American education. In 1995, the National Assessment of Educational Progress (NAEP), an arm of the U.S. Department of Education that monitors academic achievement through periodic testing of 4th, 8th, and 12th graders, reported that barely 36 percent of 12th graders, only 31 percent of 8th graders, and fewer than half of all 4th graders could read at the proficient level. By the 4th grade, 100 percent of students should be testing at or above basic skills level, but the latest NAEP reading test results showed that the state with the highest percentage (Maine) had only 75 percent of 4th grade students at or above that level. The results also suggested a downward trend: In 1994, 12th grade students performed more poorly in reading than in 1992.

It's no longer safe to assume that everything must be okay if your child continues to be promoted, as there is often an unpublicized "no-fail" policy in schools, where children are routinely advanced to the next grade when they have not achieved even a remedial level in the previous grade. The thinking was that "flunking" stigmatized a child and separated him from his peer group, and that the child would continue to do poorly and possibly end up not graduating. It was deemed preferable to put a child into the next grade and give additional academic support. Unfortunately, this support was not always available, but the policy was in place and the child would be passed along nonetheless. So how do you make sure that your child is on the right track—that he doesn't become a part of these bleak statistics?

You *can* identify specific learning problems by checking the results of whatever standardized test your child is required to take in school every year. But these tests vary from state to state, and not all teachers support the findings. Part of the problem is that America, unlike most advanced nations, does not have a national curriculum. The states' constitutional right to establish their own educational systems means that some schools have a wonderful school curriculum, but others leave much to be desired. It also means that students' annual standardized test scores might only reflect their performance on a regional level. The American Federation of Teachers (AFT) issued "Making Standards Matter 1996," an annual 50-state report on efforts to raise academic standards. Nearly every state is working to set common academic standards for its students, but the

AFT report makes it clear that most states have more work to do to strengthen their standards. For example, at this time, there are only 15 states with standards in all four core categories (English, Math, Science, and Social Studies) that are clear, specific, and well-grounded in content. For a report on an individual state, go online for the AFT state-by-state analysis. The URL is www.aft.org//research/reports/standard/iv.htm.

Furthermore, school report cards only indicate your child's *overall* performance in reading, writing, and arithmetic. If you see a low grade in reading on your 2nd grader's report card, you only know that there's a problem—not what the problem is. You can, of course, schedule a conference with the teacher, but if the teacher is simply not conversant in phonics or reading levels, it will be difficult to isolate the problem.

But what if you could somehow figure out that your 2nd grader knows consonants and blends, but doesn't understand the difference between a long and a short vowel? This is what *How Well Does Your Child Read?* can help you do. Then, you can work with your child to remedy the problem—with workbooks, discussions, games, and exercises.

Why I wrote this book

As a parent, I had the same concerns you do. When my son was in the 1st grade, I began to suspect that he was not reading as well as he should have been. When my son's teacher was not able to provide much concrete information about why, I had him tested at the local Sylvan Learning Center.

The test was a simple, straightforward inventory of the basic skills involved in phonics and reading. I realized that something like this could be used by a parent to monitor a child's reading skills on an ongoing basis. As a linguist and the director of American Accent Training—a nationwide program to teach foreign-born students to speak standard American English—I had experience creating diagnostic speech analyses and grammar and accent tests. I used what I knew about linguistic development and created a phonics "inventory" to test my own son, as well as the children in the ACE (After Class Enrichment) Program I had founded at the local elementary school.

This became the foundation for *How Well Does Your Child Read?* and led me to write two more books featuring tests to help you assess your child's performance: *How Well Does Your Child Write?* and *How Well Does Your Child Do Math?*.

The material for my diagnostic tests has been garnered from a number of reliable sources. I studied the NAEP's assessments of American students' abilities in reading, mathematics, and writing. It has been conducting such tests since 1969, ranking the results of the tests by state and providing appropriate achievement goals for each age and grade. I also relied on books on test research; advice from the former director of Sylvan Learning Centers; and online information from the U.S. Department of Education, the American Federation of Teachers, Regional Educational Laboratories, and the ERIC Clearinghouses. Finally, my diagnostic tests went through a series of trial runs with children, in addition to being evaluated by experienced elementary school teachers and reviewed by an educational therapist.

How to use this book

How Well Does Your Child Read? contains a phonics and reading diagnostic/placement test for children in kindergarten through grade 5. It will help you determine to which grade level your child has mastered phonics and reading. You can use this assessment to target areas that may need additional work. Or if it shows that your child is performing at or above his grade level, this book can allay your doubts about your child's ability and help you guide him into the next level.

The book contains the following sections:

♦ A learning style pre-test to determine whether your child's learning style is primarily auditory (does your child acquire and retain information by what he hears?) or visual (does he acquire and retain information by what he sees?) (pages 23-24).

♦ A phonics assessment, testing knowledge of the alphabet (including upper and lower case); letter and sound correspondence (26 letters, 32 sounds); consonant blends (*st, tr, bl*); digraphs (*th, sh, ch, wh, ph*); long and short vowels; clusters (*str, spl*); double consonants; double vowels; word endings; and sight words (words that cannot be sounded out) (pages 29-52).

♦ A reading assessment, testing kindergartners on perception of story order and story sense (using pictures) and children in grades 1-5 on identification of the main idea and conclusion, finding details, and context (pages 53-84).

◆ Charts to help you track your child's progress (phonics chart on page 52; reading chart on pages 85-86).

◆ A chapter on grade level guidelines for kindergarten through 5th grade (pages 87-140).

◆ A reading reassessment (pages 141-172).

◆ An explanation of the NAEP's latest reading assessment, with a chart showing the performance of individual states (pages 175-177).

◆ Appendices containing listings of educational support centers and online resources (pages 179-186).

◆ A listing of 500 high-frequency words (pages 110 and 187-188).

The phonics assessment

For many years, teachers used the phonics method—in which rules governing the sound of a letter were used to sound out words—to teach reading, writing, and spelling. For example, *pet* has a short *e* sound because it is a one-syllable word ending in *t*. *Pete* has a long *e* sound because of the silent *e* at the end of the word. Phonics dealt with exceptions to these rules as *sight words*—words that don't look the way they sound, such as *laugh* or *thought*. Students learned these irregular words and memorized their spelling. But in recent years, educators came to prefer the whole language teaching method over phonics. The proponents of whole language felt that if children were exposed to literature, by being read to and having good books available, they would pick up the rules as they went along.

Some students *do* learn to read well with whole language. On the other hand, other students are faced with frustration and failure when they try to learn to read without the ability to break a word down into sounds and put them together for meaning. The study of phonics gives students "decoding" skills that enable them to sound words out.

Educators are now coming to the conclusion that the phonics and whole language debate is not a matter of "either/or." Phonics is the first logical step, followed by exposure to literature.

This, then, is how the diagnostic test in this book is organized—phonics first, reading second. Letter sounds need to be mastered—typically by the end of 1st grade—before your child can go on to the reading section. Therefore, each set of words in the phonics section requires an 80 percent accuracy rate. For example, if on a test page five sounds are tested, one mistake is acceptable, but two mistakes would mean your child had gotten only 60 percent correct. At this point, stop the test. Spend some time at home helping your child study the sounds on that page. You can try flash cards, letter games, or pointing out particular sounds when you read to your child. When you feel your child understands the information fully, you can give the test again.

The sound of a consonant (*b* or *t* or *m*) can be pronounced alone, but vowels need to be within the context of a word in order to distinguish between long and short vowels (for example, *mate* and *mat*). Therefore, in the phonics test, all vowel sounds are tested within words.

Most of the words used in the phonics test have been invented—for example, *wug* or *glav*. Invented words are helpful because your child will not have already memorized their pronunciations without first understanding the underlying rule—the way he might have with real words like *bag* or *glove*. Invented words can test whether your child really understands the rules or not. If a child sees *glav* and says "glav" with a short *a* sound, he has truly sounded out the word according to the rules of regular spelling. However, if he answers "glave" with a long *a* sound, you'll know he needs to practice the short *a* sound.

Scoring the phonics assessment

In the phonics assessment, mark a ✓ for correct answers and an ✖ for incorrect answers. Though it may seem quicker to mark only the incorrect answers, doing this might cause your child to react negatively and dispute your scoring, possibly slowing down the test.

As you give the phonics test, check the bottom of each page for the allowable number of ✖'s, which will vary between 1 and 5, depending on the number of items in the section. For example:

> 0 to 1 ✖ enter date in chart on page 52 and go to the next page; 2 or more ✖'s, stop test and go to Guidelines on page 87. Retest at a later date.

Do not go past the point where your child exceeds the allowable number of errors. Each time a particular test has been completed, note the date in the chart on page on page 52.

With each word your child has to pronounce in the phonics test, he may respond in one of four ways, which you would mark as follows:

Answers immediately and correctly	✓
Hesitates, then gives the correct answer	✘
Fails to respond	✘
Gives an incorrect response.	✘

Only the first type of response—an immediate and correct answer—will be considered the correct response.

If your child hesitates—that is, doesn't give the correct pronunciation *spontaneously*—you should write an ✘ in the corresponding box, even if your child does eventually give the right response. It is extremely important that your child answer immediately for the answer to be correct, because any hesitation means that he may be familiar with the sound or word, but has not mastered it.

It is also helpful for you to write down what your child actually said, as you can use this after the test to diagnose and practice vowels that your child has difficulty with.

Remember that a child can get the targeted sound (a vowel sound, for example) correct even if an untargeted sound (a consonant sound, for example) is wrong. From page 34 on, you are only listening for the targeted sound. For example, if you are targeting the long *a* sound in *later*, but your child immediately answers, "*tater*," the targeted vowel sound—a long *a*—is still correct. Mark a ✓ and write what your child actually said on the line. (This will be useful for diagnosing problems with certain consonants.) On the other hand, if your child answers *hopping* when the answer should have been *hoping*, he did not give the targeted sound—the long *o* sound—and you should mark an ✘.

There's no need to use a timer to measure how long your child pauses. Simply remember that a child needs to know phonics *cold*, and any hesitation means that a particular phonics skill has not been *mastered*. Because every child is different, you can define hesitation as when he breaks his own pace. If your child is stumped and doesn't respond, mark an ✖.

The reading assessment

After successful completion of the phonics section, give your child the reading test. If your child is a more advanced reader, you may be tempted to skip the phonics section and the early reading sections, but don't. Letting your child see just how much he already knows can be a great motivator. When your child starts to slow down or miss answers, he will have already gotten a sense of achievement.

For kindergartners, the reading test is made up of sets of pictures, rather than words, that tell a story. This section tests the kindergartner's grasp of story order by asking him to number four pictures in the order in which the scenes were most likely to have occurred. It will also test story sense, by presenting two pictures and then asking your child to point out which of two other scenes is most likely to happen next. At the kindergarten level, speed is not important—you are checking to see if the answer is correct.

The kindergarten pre-reading tests will tell you if your child needs work on logic, sequencing, or matching, as well as context and details.

For 1st grade through 5th grade, the reading section tests context and vocabulary, fact checking, finding the main idea, and drawing a conclusion. You will evaluate your child on the following four criteria:

1. **Fluency:** How smoothly did your child read? Was the reading choppy, halting, or disjointed? Was it smooth and flowing? Did the intonation reflect the punctuation and the meaning?
2. **Speed:** Did it take less than a minute or more than a minute?
3. **Vocabulary:** Were there more than three unknown words? Fewer than three?
4. **Response:** Was the response correct or incorrect?

Reading	❏ fluent	❏ halting
Speed	❏ less than 1 minute	❏ more than 1 minute
Vocabulary	❏ 0-3 unknown words	❏ 3+ unknown words
Response	❏ correct	❏ incorrect

In the reading assessment, it's okay for your child to look back over the text or picture for the answer. This part of the assessment is for comprehension, not memory.

An important distinction in assessing reading skills is the difference between *comprehension* and *fluency*. A child may read haltingly, but understand the material at the end, whereas another child may read beautifully, and have no idea of the content. The reading assessment will let you know what to work on.

During the reading main idea and conclusion assessments, mark the bottom of each page for your child's performance. These guidelines let you know your child's reading strengths and weaknesses. The first three categories—reading, speed, and vocabulary—are not critical for trying the next grade level. On the other hand, comprehension *is* critical. So if your child misses either a main idea or conclusion question, or goes beyond the acceptable number of errors for context or fact finding, the reading test should stop at that grade level.

Generally speaking, the more times a child reads a text, the more smoothly and fluently he will read. And once he is told the answer, he will remember it— independent of increased comprehension. Because of this, when you re-test the child, the reading selections must be taken from the back of the book and, unlike the phonics section, not simply repeated.

Is this an intelligence test?

No. It is extremely important to remember that early or late reading is not an indicator of intelligence. Phonics skills and the reading level will tell you the skill range or level a child has acquired *at that certain point.* Late readers can be given the tools and develop into great readers. Early readers may develop other, stronger interests. In either case, however, children need to be helped through the transition from phonics and basic comprehension, to enjoying and relating to literature and reading.

Before you begin

Before you plunge into the rest of this book, are you sure that no physical or learning impediments are hampering your child's ability to read? For example, has your child's eyesight been checked recently? If he has been displaying learning problems, have you ruled out the possibility of Attention Deficit Disorder (ADD) or dyslexia? Only after you've determined that your child is ready, willing, and *able* to learn should you give the diagnostic test to determine what your child's reading level is and what you may do to improve it.

How to give the test

Set aside 20 minutes alone with your child in a quiet room. Make sure there are no distractions—turn off the TV, and never try to give this test just before a big soccer match or gymnastics practice.

Tell your child this will only take a few minutes and that the results will help him enjoy reading more. Stress that there's no pressure, no punishment, no failing.

Depending on the age of your child, the two of you can sit side-by-side while you score and he answers the questions. Direct your child's attention to the words on the page, not the marks you're making. Some children can become anxious if they pay too much attention to your scoring.

Students in kindergarten through 2nd grade should be monitored closely because they cannot always read the instructions, and they will have a greater tendency to get sidetracked. Independent study starts in the 3rd grade, so children at the 3rd grade level or higher can have greater autonomy during the test. (Of course, the behavior of individual children can vary greatly, so there will be exceptions to this.)

For kindergartners, the test will take from one minute (because they don't know the alphabet well) to 20 minutes. I recommend a 20-minute limit to combat the "fatigue factor" as boredom or exasperation can lower children's scores even in subjects they know well. Children in 1st through 5th grade should finish the test within 20 minutes.

What if your child takes longer? Well, phonics skills need to be quick and accurate. If your child takes too much time on the phonics section, he doesn't know the material. At that point, the test should be stopped, and the previous lessons drilled. On the other hand, it's okay if your child goes over the allotted time with the reading selections as long as he is giving the correct responses. The critical factor in that section is comprehension, not speed.

What to do after the test

Once your child reaches the point in the test where the questions are beyond his grade level, you can end the test. Turn to the scoring section and determine the grade level that corresponds to your child's score. Once that has been determined, consult the chapter on standards for each grade level—kindergarten through 5th. Here you will find suggestions on helping your child with any areas of difficulty that have been identified in the assessment. These standards and guidelines can help you with remediation if your child scores below grade level. This chapter also introduces you to the next level or levels if your child is at or above grade level.

One of the primary functions of the test is to familiarize you with the materials that should be taught at each level. Once that familiarization has taken place, you can seek out appropriate materials for your child.

Children like to be read to from higher-level books, but when reading themselves, they need books that are interesting and challenging, not overwhelming. Also, it's okay if your child wants to read the same easy book over and over. That's an excellent way to reinforce the basics and build reading confidence and fluency.

Spelling and pronunciation drills can also become part of the remediation work you'll do with your child. You can use flash cards to reinforce your kindergartner's knowledge of sight words and of two- or three-letter, short vowel, phonetic words. This includes words such as *pat, sat, hat; it, bit, sit; in, tin,* and *fin.* For children in 1st grade and up, you can make lists of words on note cards for spelling drills. Call Matrix at 800-457-4255 to obtain the flash cards that are appropriate to your child's level.

Retesting

If you feel your child has made progress after the work you've done together, you can test him again. Or even if he performed at the appropriate level the first time around, you still may want to give the test periodically to monitor skills. In the first case, your child needs to be tested at the same level as before, but he may have memorized the answers, so use the reassessments in the back of the book. In the second scenario, you can just pick up at the point in the test where your child left off.

Each time you give the test, record the date so you can chart your child's progress. Continue monitoring until your child is at or above grade level.

How often should you retest your child? This depends upon the age of the child. A 5-year-old who is just learning his letters could be tested every four months, while a 7-year-old, who needs to master the concepts for school, could be tested every two months. Children who are on track could be tested at the beginning and end of each school year.

Now, if you're ready (and your child is ready), let's find out how well your child can read!

Learning Style Pre-test

It is helpful for parents to understand a child's learning style. Some children's learning strength is *auditory*—they acquire and retain information by what they hear; others learn *visually*—by what they see; and some children learn the best in a *tactile* or *kinesthetic* way—by physically touching or manipulating the objects that they are counting.

This quick test will help determine if your child's learning style is markedly auditory or visual.

Auditory Sequential Memory

Tell your child the objects shown in each set at a rate of one every two seconds. Then ask her to repeat the list back. Keep adding a new object to the set until she makes a mistake.

1. 📫 ☎ ✂
2. ☎ 📖 🔔 ✏
3. 📖 ☎ ✏ 🕐 🔔
4. ☎ ✂ ✏ 📖 🕐 ★
5. 🔔 📫 ✂ ✏ 🕐 ★ 📖

Visual Sequential Memory

Show the set of objects to your child, allowing two seconds for each object in a set. Then remove or cover the paper and ask her to list the objects she saw. Keep adding a new set until she makes a mistake.

1. 🕐 ★ 🔔

2. ✈ ✂ ☺ ☎

3. 🔔 ★ 📬 📖 〰

4. ✈ ✂ 🕐 🔔 ☺ ✏

5. 📖 ☎ ✂ ✏ 🕐 ★ 📬

Interpretation

Most people use a combination of learning styles, but usually one is dominant. If your child shows a marked preference for *visual memory*, she would benefit by practicing reading skills with flash cards and pictures.

If your child shows a marked preference for *auditory memory*, she would benefit by practicing out loud—chanting the alphabet, reciting simple word spellings, or listening to tapes.

A child with a marked preference for *kinesthetic memory* would benefit by practicing with manipulatives—blocks, word matching exercises, and making her own flash cards.

The main point is that not all approaches work for all children. Experiment with different approaches and see what works best for your child.

Test-taking Techniques

There are two elements to taking a test successfully. Most important, of course, is knowing the information. The other is knowing the test.

Tests are written according to basic standards and practices. This is why school tests are called *standardized*. It is very helpful for your child to be familiar with test standards and formats before starting a test, so that she can focus on the content, rather than on the test itself. Here are some basic guidelines:

First, look the whole test over. This includes noting how much time you have for the test, how long the test is, and what kind of test it is—multiple choice, fill-in-the-blank, essay, or a combination of the three. Many a 10-year-old has gotten to the end of a test with 10 minutes left to go, only to be dismayed to find two essay questions tucked away at the end of the test.

Next, put your pencil down and read the instructions. Then read them again.

After you read each instruction set, look for *key words* that tell you what kind of writing is needed (*describe, explain, persuade*), the specific facts you need (*who, what, where, when, why, how*), or the sequence of events (*first, then, next, at last, finally*). Notice if there are any negative words in the instructions (Which word is *not* a noun?) or if the question asks for *similarities* or *opposites*.

Make sure that you know exactly what you are supposed to be looking for in the text. If you are supposed to find the *main idea*, you have to read the entire passage and think about what the most important point was; whereas if you are looking for *details*, you can scan the passage to find the exact fact. Read all the questions before you read the passage—that way you'll know what you're looking for while you are reading. Be sure to underline the answers in the passage rather than trying to rely on your memory. Circle any words that you aren't sure of and try to figure them out by the context.

Following this, prioritize to determine if questions are equally weighted. If some questions are worth only 1 point and others are worth 10 points, spend more time and energy on the more heavily weighted problems.

If there are questions you just don't know the answer to, don't spend time agonizing over them. Move on to the questions you are familiar with, then go back to the ones you're less sure of.

One of the easiest techniques for a multiple choice test is the process of elimination. If there are four possibilities, chances are that one of them will be way off base, so first, eliminate the ridiculous. Another one will probably be fairly unlikely. Cross that one out, too. Of the two remaining, both will be possibilities, but since you've eliminated the clearly wrong answers, you can concentrate on finding the correct one of two, instead of the correct one of four. For example, here's a question from a typical 3rd grade standardized test:

Mark the answer with the correct punctuation.

Thanksgiving is always on a _____

- ❏ Thursday.
- ❏ Thursday!
- ❏ Thursday,
- ❏ Thursday

When you read it all together, "Thanksgiving is always on a Thursday," you can say that it is a complete sentence. Because it is a complete sentence, it needs an end mark. Hence, the last answer—*Thursday*—can be eliminated. From there, look at the sentence and ask yourself, "Is it a question? Is it the middle of a sentence?" This will eliminate *Thursday?* and *Thursday,* leaving *Thursday.*—which is the correct answer. Now that you've figured this question out, look for others that are similar to it.

When taking a multiple choice test, when you just don't know the answer, always take a guess from the answers you deem most likely to be correct. If you have four choices from which to choose, you have a 25 percent chance of getting the correct answer, and if you've narrowed those four choices down to two possible answers, then you have a 50 percent chance of getting the right answer.

On page 28 you will find a list of test-taking tips that you can keep handy for reviewing with your child, especially when she is preparing to take a test.

Test-taking tips

1. Look the whole test over.
2. Prioritize.
3. Read the instructions.
4. Read the instructions again.
5. Make sure that you have scratch paper for notes and outlines.
6. Look for key words.
7. Make sure that you know what you are looking for in the passage.
8. Make sure that you check all possible answers before you choose one. Don't choose the first one that looks likely.
9. Look for similar types of problems.
10. Review the test and complete any answers you may have skipped.

Phonics Assessment

Kindergarten and First Grade

Alphabet Upper Case   *Kindergarten*

Say each letter. Start with **Z** and work back to **A**.

	✓	✗	notes		✓	✗	notes
Z	☐	☐	_____	M	☐	☐	_____
Y	☐	☐	_____	L	☐	☐	_____
X	☐	☐	_____	K	☐	☐	_____
W	☐	☐	_____	J	☐	☐	_____
V	☐	☐	_____	I	☐	☐	_____
U	☐	☐	_____	H	☐	☐	_____
T	☐	☐	_____	G	☐	☐	_____
S	☐	☐	_____	F	☐	☐	_____
R	☐	☐	_____	E	☐	☐	_____
Q	☐	☐	_____	D	☐	☐	_____
P	☐	☐	_____	C	☐	☐	_____
O	☐	☐	_____	B	☐	☐	_____
N	☐	☐	_____	A	☐	☐	_____

✓ = immediate response   ✗ = slow or incorrect response
0 to 5 ✗'s enter date in chart on page 52 and go to the next page; 6 or more ✗'s, stop test and go to Guidelines on page 87. Retest at a later date.

Alphabet Lower Case　　　　　*Kindergarten*

Say each letter. Start with **z** and work back to **a**.

	✓	✗	notes		✓	✗	notes
z	☐	☐	_____	m	☐	☐	_____
y	☐	☐	_____	l	☐	☐	_____
x	☐	☐	_____	k	☐	☐	_____
w	☐	☐	_____	j	☐	☐	_____
v	☐	☐	_____	i	☐	☐	_____
u	☐	☐	_____	h	☐	☐	_____
t	☐	☐	_____	g	☐	☐	_____
s	☐	☐	_____	f	☐	☐	_____
r	☐	☐	_____	e	☐	☐	_____
q	☐	☐	_____	d	☐	☐	_____
p	☐	☐	_____	c	☐	☐	_____
o	☐	☐	_____	b	☐	☐	_____
n	☐	☐	_____	a	☐	☐	_____

✓ = immediate response　　✗ = slow or incorrect response
0 to 5 ✗'s enter date in chart on page 52 and go to the next
page; 6 or more ✗'s, stop test and go to Guidelines on page
87. Retest at a later date.

Consonants

Make the **sound** of each letter below (not the *name*—for example, *buh*, not *bee*).

	✓	✗	notes		✓	✗	notes
b	☐	☐	_____	p	☐	☐	_____
c*	☐	☐	_____	q	☐	☐	_____
d	☐	☐	_____	r	☐	☐	_____
f	☐	☐	_____	s	☐	☐	_____
g*	☐	☐	_____	t	☐	☐	_____
h	☐	☐	_____	v	☐	☐	_____
j	☐	☐	_____	w	☐	☐	_____
k	☐	☐	_____	x	☐	☐	_____
l	☐	☐	_____	y	☐	☐	_____
m	☐	☐	_____	z	☐	☐	_____
n	☐	☐	_____				

*These letters have two sounds each. (See pp. 117)

> ✓ = immediate response   ✗ = slow or incorrect response
> 0 to 4 ✗'s enter date in chart on page 52 and go to the next page; 5 or more ✗'s, stop test and go to Guidelines on page 87. Retest at a later date.

Sight Words

First Grade

Read the following words.

	✓	✗	notes
a	☐	☐	_____
I	☐	☐	_____
is	☐	☐	_____
an	☐	☐	_____
and	☐	☐	_____
the	☐	☐	_____

✓ = immediate response   ✗ = slow or incorrect response
0 to 1 ✗ enter date in chart on page 52 and go to the next page; 2 or more ✗'s, stop test and go to Guidelines on page 87. Retest at a later date.

Short Vowels

The phonics words from this point on contain nonsense syllables, so you can accurately hear the changing vowels. From this page forward, you are only listening for the targeted vowel sound. If the consonant sound is wrong, but the vowel is correct, mark ✓. However, do write the actual word your child says on the line so you can determine which consonant sounds he has trouble with. Read the following words.

		✓	✗	notes
A	wag	☐	☐	_____
E	weg	☐	☐	_____
I	wig	☐	☐	_____
O	wog	☐	☐	_____
U	wug	☐	☐	_____

✓ = immediate response   ✗ = slow or incorrect response
0 to 1 ✗ enter date in chart on page 52 and go to the next page; 2 or more ✗'s, stop test and go to Guidelines on page 87. Retest at a later date.

Consonant Blends   *First Grade*

Here are **blends** at the beginning of a word. Read the following words.

		✓	✗	notes
BL	blan	☐	☐	_____
BR	brog	☐	☐	_____
PL	plep	☐	☐	_____
PR	prot	☐	☐	_____
CL	clin	☐	☐	_____
CR	cret	☐	☐	_____
DR	drid	☐	☐	_____
TR	trop	☐	☐	_____
ST	steg	☐	☐	_____

✓ = immediate response   ✗ = slow or incorrect response
0 to 2 ✗'s enter date in chart on page 52 and go to the next page; 3 or more ✗'s, stop test and go to Guidelines on page 87. Retest at a later date.

Sight Words   *First Grade*

Read the following words.

	✓	✗	notes
to	☐	☐	_____
go	☐	☐	_____
do	☐	☐	_____
by	☐	☐	_____
or	☐	☐	_____
of	☐	☐	_____
as	☐	☐	_____
he	☐	☐	_____
she	☐	☐	_____
for	☐	☐	_____
say	☐	☐	_____
from	☐	☐	_____

✓ = immediate response   ✗ = slow or incorrect response
0 to 2 ✗'s enter date in chart on page 52 and go to the next
page; 3 or more ✗'s, stop test and go to Guidelines on page
87. Retest at a later date.

Consonant Digraphs   *First Grade*

There is an important distinction between a blend and a digraph. A blend can be *sounded out (bl)*, whereas a digraph uses two letters to form one new sound *(sh)*. In other words, you can't sound out a digraph. Here are consonant digraphs at the beginning of a word. Read the following words.

		✓	✗	notes
WH	whep	☐	☐	_____
TH	tham	☐	☐	_____
SH	shog	☐	☐	_____
CH	chun	☐	☐	_____
PH	pheb	☐	☐	_____

✓ = immediate response   ✗ = slow or incorrect response
0 to 1 ✗ enter date in chart on page 52 and go to the next page; 2 or more ✗'s, stop test and go to Guidelines on page 87. Retest at a later date.

Ending Digraphs   *First Grade*

Here are consonant digraphs at the end of a word. Read the following words.

	✓	✗	notes
sith	☐	☐	_____
gach	☐	☐	_____
lish	☐	☐	_____
taph	☐	☐	_____

✓ = immediate response   ✗ = slow or incorrect response
0 to 1 ✗ enter date in chart on page 52 and go to the next
page; 2 or more ✗'s, stop test and go to Guidelines on page
87. Retest at a later date.

Long Vowels

A silent *e* after the consonant makes a vowel long. Read the following words.

	✓	✗	notes
vate	☐	☐	_____
rete	☐	☐	_____
fime	☐	☐	_____
pote	☐	☐	_____
kue	☐	☐	_____

✓ = immediate response   ✗ = slow or incorrect response
0 to 1 ✗ enter date in chart on page 52 and go to the next page; 2 or more ✗'s, stop test and go to Guidelines on page 87. Retest at a later date.

Sight Words

First Grade

Read the following words.

	✓	✗	notes
what	☐	☐	_____
have	☐	☐	_____
saw	☐	☐	_____
was	☐	☐	_____
they	☐	☐	_____
there	☐	☐	_____
one	☐	☐	_____
some	☐	☐	_____
you	☐	☐	_____
your	☐	☐	_____
are	☐	☐	_____
does	☐	☐	_____
don't	☐	☐	_____
done	☐	☐	_____
gone	☐	☐	_____

✓ = immediate response ✗ = slow or incorrect response
0 to 3 ✗'s enter date in chart on page 52 and go to the next page; 4 or more ✗'s, stop test and go to Guidelines on page 87. Retest at a later date.

Sight Words   *First Grade*

Read the following words.

	✓	✗	notes
good	☐	☐	_____
right	☐	☐	_____
often	☐	☐	_____
another	☐	☐	_____
why	☐	☐	_____
again	☐	☐	_____
every	☐	☐	_____
away	☐	☐	_____
along	☐	☐	_____
until	☐	☐	_____
going	☐	☐	_____
while	☐	☐	_____
both	☐	☐	_____
because	☐	☐	_____
few	☐	☐	_____

✓ = immediate response   ✗ = slow or incorrect response
0 to 3 ✗'s enter date in chart on page 52 and go to the next
page; 4 or more ✗'s, stop test and go to Guidelines on page
87. Retest at a later date.

Long Vowels   *First Grade*

In addition to the long vowels made by the silent *e* (for example, *not* becomes *note* with the silent *e*), there are other important long vowel sounds. Read the following words.

		✓	✗	notes
A	cray	☐	☐	_____
	dail	☐	☐	_____
E	neen	☐	☐	_____
	leat	☐	☐	_____
I	bly	☐	☐	_____
	snyle	☐	☐	_____
O	hoat	☐	☐	_____
	dold	☐	☐	_____
U	hoon	☐	☐	_____
	tew	☐	☐	_____

✓ = immediate response   ✗ = slow or incorrect response
0 to 2 ✗'s enter date in chart on page 52 and go to the next page; 3 or more ✗'s, stop test and go to Guidelines on page 87. Retest at a later date.

Sight Words   *First Grade*

Read the following words.

	✓	✗	notes
people	☐	☐	_____
heard	☐	☐	_____
heart	☐	☐	_____
sure	☐	☐	_____
honest	☐	☐	_____
beautiful	☐	☐	_____
busy	☐	☐	_____
cover	☐	☐	_____
move	☐	☐	_____
huge	☐	☐	_____

> ✓ = immediate response   ✗ = slow or incorrect response
> 0 to 2 ✗'s enter date in chart on page 52 and go to the next
> page; 3 or more ✗'s, stop test and go to Guidelines on page
> 87. Retest at a later date.

Ending Blends

First Grade

Read the following words.

	✓	✗	notes
moggle	☐	☐	_____
tepple	☐	☐	_____
lomble	☐	☐	_____
mardle	☐	☐	_____
riffle	☐	☐	_____
tottle	☐	☐	_____
beckle	☐	☐	_____
fengle	☐	☐	_____
sancle	☐	☐	_____
vample	☐	☐	_____

✓= immediate response   ✗ = slow or incorrect response
0 to 2 ✗'s enter date in chart on page 52 and go to the next page; 3 or more ✗'s, stop test and go to Guidelines on page 87. Retest at a later date.

Consonant Clusters

First Grade

After consonant blends, there are consonant clusters—three consonants together. Blends can occur at the beginning, middle, or end of a word. Clusters only occur at the beginning or middle of a word. They do not occur at the end. Read the following words.

		✓	✗	notes
THR	threm	☐	☐	_____
SHR	shrup	☐	☐	_____
CHR	chren	☐	☐	_____
SCR	scrim	☐	☐	_____
STR	strub	☐	☐	_____
SPR	spron	☐	☐	_____
SPL	splif	☐	☐	_____
SQU	squog	☐	☐	_____

✓ = immediate response ✗ = slow or incorrect response
0 to 2 ✗'s enter date in chart on page 52 and go to the next page; 3 or more ✗'s, stop test and go to Guidelines on page 87. Retest at a later date.

Double Consonants *First Grade*

Double consonants make a vowel short. Read the following words.

	✓	✗	notes
gatter	☐	☐	_____
tetter	☐	☐	_____
finner	☐	☐	_____
nopping	☐	☐	_____
lupper	☐	☐	_____

Short and Long Vowels   *First Grade*

This exercise contrasts words with and without a final *e*.
Read the following pairs of words.

	✓	✗	notes
dat	☐	☐	_____
date	☐	☐	_____
ret	☐	☐	_____
rete	☐	☐	_____
lin	☐	☐	_____
line	☐	☐	_____
nop	☐	☐	_____
nope	☐	☐	_____
ruk	☐	☐	_____
ruke	☐	☐	_____

✓ = immediate response   ✗ = slow or incorrect response
0 to 2 ✗'s enter date in chart on page 52 and go to the next page; 3 or more ✗'s, stop test and go to Guidelines on page 87. Retest at a later date.

Single and Double Consonants *First Grade*

This exercise contrasts double and single consonants. Read the following pairs of words.

	✓	✗	notes
datter	☐	☐	_____
dater	☐	☐	_____
remmer	☐	☐	_____
remer	☐	☐	_____
finner	☐	☐	_____
finer	☐	☐	_____
topping	☐	☐	_____
toping	☐	☐	_____
bupper	☐	☐	_____
buper	☐	☐	_____

✓ = immediate response ✗ = slow or incorrect response
0 to 2 ✗'s enter date in chart on page 52 and go to the next page; 3 or more ✗'s, stop test and go to Guidelines on page 87. Retest at a later date.

R-Controlled Vowels   *First Grade*

Here are different vowels in combination with the letter *R*. Read the following words.

	✓	✗	notes
mirt	☐	☐	_____
nurm	☐	☐	_____
lerg	☐	☐	_____
garp	☐	☐	_____
porf	☐	☐	_____

✓ = immediate response   ✗ = slow or incorrect response
0 to 1 ✗ enter date in chart on page 52 and go to the next page; 2 or more ✗'s, stop test and go to Guidelines on page 87. Retest at a later date.

Endings

These endings indicate consistent and accepted *changes in meaning*, such as the *-ed* ending for the past tense or *-er* for comparatives or to indicate a person who does something (e.g. *reader*). Read the following words.

	✓	✗	notes
wugged	☐	☐	_____
tudding	☐	☐	_____
lagger	☐	☐	_____
ribby	☐	☐	_____
ribbier	☐	☐	_____

These double consonant endings indicate the pronunciation of a short vowel sound. Read the following words.

nuck	☐	☐	_____
senk	☐	☐	_____
ting	☐	☐	_____
wint	☐	☐	_____
bolm	☐	☐	_____

✓ = immediate response   ✗ = slow or incorrect response
0 to 2 ✗'s enter date in chart on page 52 and go to the next page; 3 or more ✗'s, stop test and go to Guidelines on page 87. Retest at a later date.

Vowel Digraphs   *First Grade*

These are the vowel combinations that make a new sound. Read the following words.

	✓	✗	notes
toog	☐	☐	_____
maut	☐	☐	_____
gain	☐	☐	_____
lound	☐	☐	_____
thew	☐	☐	_____

✓ = immediate response   ✗ = slow or incorrect response
0 to 1 ✗ enter date in chart on page 52 and go to the next page; 2 or more ✗'s, stop test and go to Guidelines on page 87. Retest at a later date.

Phonics Record

As you give your child the phonics test, check the bottom of the page for the allowable number of errors. The goal is a minimum of 80 percent accuracy. Once your child has mastered a phonics skill, note the date in the chart below.

Date Passed	Phonics Skill	Level
	Alphabet Upper Case	Kindergarten
	Alphabet Lower Case	
	Consonant Sounds	Early 1st grade
	Sight Words	
	Short Vowels	
	Consonant Blends	
	Sight Words	Mid 1st grade
	Consonant Digraphs	
	Ending Digraphs	
	Long Vowels	
	Sight Words *(pages 40-41)*	
	Long Vowels	Late 1st grade
	Sight Words	
	Ending Blends	
	Consonant Clusters	
	Double Consonants	
	Short & Long Vowels (silent *e*)	
	Single & Double Consonants	
	R-Controlled Vowels	End 1st grade
	Endings	
	Vowel Digraphs	

Reading Assessment

Kindergarten through Fifth Grade

Matching Pictures   *Kindergarten*

Look at the picture on the left. Draw a circle around the matching picture in the box.

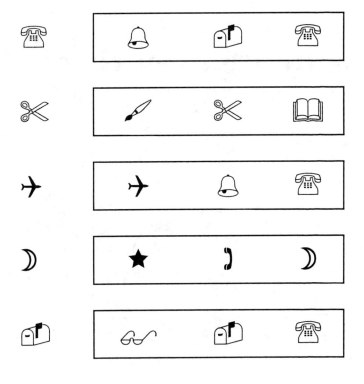

0-1 ✖, enter date in chart on page 85 and go to the next page; 2 or more ✖'s, go to Guidelines on page 87 and retest at a later date.

Matching Letters

Look at the letter on the left. Draw a circle around the matching letter in the box.

W | T   P   W |

B | A   B   P |

L | M   I   L |

U | U   V   X |

Z | B   Z   Y |

0-1 ✘, enter date in chart on page 85 and go to the next page; 2 or more ✘'s, go to Guidelines on page 87 and retest at a later date.

Context

Circle the picture that best finishes each sentence.

The boy jumped into the

 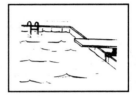

The cat chased the

The girl hugged her

0-1 ✖, enter date in chart on page 85 and go to the next page; 2 or more ✖'s, go to Guidelines on page 87 and retest at a later date.

Fact Finding

Look at the picture and tell if each sentence is TRUE or FALSE.

	True	**False**
1. The dog is jumping rope.	❏	❏
2. There are six animals in the picture.	❏	❏
3. There are more cats than dogs.	❏	❏

0-1 ✘, enter date in chart on page 85 and go to the next page; 2 or more ✘'s, go to Guidelines on page 87 and retest at a later date.

Story Order   *Kindergarten*

Look at the four pictures. Decide what order they should
be in to tell a story. Write numbers 1 to 4 in the little
boxes to show the order.

Correct order, enter date in chart on page 85 and go to the
next page; incorrect order, stop test and go to Guidelines
on page 87. Restest at a later date.

Story Sense

Look at the top pictures. Draw a circle around the bottom box that shows what is more likely to happen next.

Correct response, enter date in chart on page 85 and go to the next page; incorrect response, stop test and go to Guidelines on page 87. Restest at a later date.

Context   *First Grade*

Choose the word that best finishes the sentence.

1. Every morning we get out of _____.

   ❑ far   ❑ bed   ❑ house

2. The dogs like to _____.

   ❑ bark   ❑ that   ❑ eats

3. Tomorrow is _____.

   ❑ Tuesday   ❑ July   ❑ hot

0-1 ✖, enter date in chart on page 85 and go on to the next page; 2 or more ✖'s, go to Guidelines on page 87 and retest at a later date.

Fact Finding

Read the following paragraph and tell if each sentence is TRUE or FALSE.

I am an animal. I have four legs. I have black and white stripes. I am a zebra. I live on the African plains.

	True	**False**
1. The animal has two legs.	❑	❑
2. The animal lives in the rain forest.	❑	❑
3. The animal is a zebra.	❑	❑

0-1 ✘, enter date in chart on page 85 and go on to the next page; 2 or more ✘'s, go to Guidelines on page 87 and retest at a later date.

Main Idea

First Grade

Read the following paragraph and answer the question that follows.

Jenny looked out the window. It was snowing. She could not go out to play. Jenny said, "I wish it would stop snowing."

The main idea is:

❑ Jenny wanted the snow to stop.

❑ Jenny liked looking at the snow.

❑ Jenny made a wish.

Reading	❑ fluent	❑ halting
Speed	❑ less than 1 minute	❑ more than 1 minute
Vocabulary	❑ 0-3 unknown words	❑ 3+ unknown words
Response	❑ correct	❑ incorrect

Correct response, enter date in chart on page 85 and go to the next page; incorrect response go to Guidelines on page 87 and retest at a later date.

Conclusions

Read the following paragraph and answer the question that follows.

Bob got out of the car. He looked at all the kids playing at the new playground. He took his cameral out of the case and adjusted the lens.

What did Bob do?

❑ Bob played at the playground.

❑ The kids played on the slide.

❑ Bob took a picture of the kids playing at the new playground.

Reading	❑ fluent	❑ halting
Speed	❑ less than 1 minute	❑ more than 1 minute
Vocabulary	❑ 0-3 unknown words	❑ 3+ unknown words
Response	❑ correct	❑ incorrect

Correct response, enter date in chart on page 85 and go to the next page; incorrect response go to Guidelines on page 87 and retest at a later date.

Context

Second Grade

Choose the word that best completes each sentence.

1. The puffer fish blows up like a balloon. It does this by taking in _____.

   ❑ trip   ❑ air   ❑ visitors

2. An elephant has a long trunk. It can _____ up to six feet long.

   ❑ fall   ❑ set   ❑ grow

3. In the olden days there were no books. Nobody knew how to _____.

   ❑ read   ❑ draw   ❑ see

4. Why don't you come to my _____?

   ❑ house   ❑ lunch   ❑ bag

5. I'm really _____ about the party.

   ❑ tired   ❑ hungry   ❑ excited

0-1 ✖, enter date in chart on page 85 and go to the next page; 2 or more ✖'s, go to Guidelines on page 87 and retest at a later date.

Fact Finding

Second Grade

Read the following paragraph and tell if each sentence is TRUE or FALSE.

Sharks are a kind of fish. They live in the ocean. They are very good swimmers. A shark does not have bones. Its skeleton is made of cartilage. There are more than 250 kinds of sharks. The biggest sharks can grow over 50 feet long.

	True	False
1. Instead of bone, sharks have cartilage.	❏	❏
2. Most sharks live in lakes.	❏	❏
3. There are about 50 different kinds of sharks.	❏	❏
4. Sharks are good swimmers.	❏	❏

0-1 ✘, enter date in chart on page 85 and go to the next page; 2 or more ✘'s, go to Guidelines on page 87 and retest at a later date.

Main Idea

Second Grade

Read the following paragraph and answer the question that follows.

A Summer Story

It is hot in summer. The sun shines and birds sing. It is nice outdoors. Most kids like to play outdoors. Some kids like to rollerblade. Some kids swim. What do you do in summer?

What is the main idea?

❑ The sun shines in summer.

❑ In summer, there are many things to do outside.

❑ It doesn't rain in the summer.

Reading	❑ fluent	❑ halting
Speed	❑ less than 1 minute	❑ more than 1 minute
Vocabulary	❑ 0-3 unknown words	❑ 3+ unknown words
Response	❑ correct	❑ incorrect

Correct response, enter date in chart on page 85 and go to the next page; incorrect response go to Guidelines on page 87 and retest at a later date.

Conclusions   *Second Grade*

Read the following paragraph and answer the questions that follow.

How to Stop a Cat Fight

Sometimes cats fight. They make loud noises. They may scratch. Do not try to pull apart fighting cats. Turn on a hose and spray them with water. This will stop the fight.

When cats fight, they

- ❏ spray
- ❏ scratch
- ❏ turn on a hose

Reading	❏ fluent	❏ halting
Speed	❏ less than 1 minute	❏ more than 1 minute
Vocabulary	❏ 0-3 unknown words	❏ 3+ unknown words
Responses	❏ correct	❏ incorrect

Correct response, enter date in chart on page 85 and go to the next page; incorrect response go to Guidelines on page 87 and retest at a later date.

Context

Third Grade

Choose the words that best complete each sentence.

1. When a person is fasting, he does not eat. People don't _____ (a) while they are sleeping, so it is like they are fasting all night. When they get up in the morning, they 'break' the _____ (b) with breakfast.

    (a) ❑ food   ❑ sleep   ❑ eat
    (b) ❑ fast   ❑ lunch   ❑ slow

2. Spider monkeys are very quick and light. They can climb easily to escape other animals or to find _____ (a). They use their hands and feet to climb— and they also use their _____(b)!

    (a) ❑ deer   ❑ self   ❑ food
    (b) ❑ ears   ❑ tails   ❑ noses

3. It is very dangerous to pick wild mushrooms. Even though they might look tasty, they can be _____ (a). Many people get _____ (b) every year from picking wild mushrooms.

    (a) ❑ delicious   ❑ danger   ❑ poisonous
    (b) ❑ lost   ❑ died   ❑ sick

4. Some people believe that it's bad _____ (a) if a black cat crosses your path. Other people think that you'll have seven years' bad luck if you break a _____ (b). In order to get rid of bad luck, you can throw salt over your shoulder or you can knock on wood.

(a) ❑ luck   ❑ idea   ❑ beliefs
(b) ❑ legs   ❑ mirror   ❑ frame

5. If you are in an open field during a thunderstorm, you might want to look for _____ (a) under a tree. Don't do this. The lightning will be attracted to the tallest thing in the area—the tree! Lie _____ (b) on the ground, instead.

(a) ❑ danger   ❑ pressure   ❑ safety
(b) ❑ over   ❑ down   ❑ off

0-2 ✗'s, enter date in chart on page 85 and go on to the next page; 3 or more ✗'s, go to Guidelines on page 87 and retest at a later date.

Fact Finding

Third Grade

Read the paragraph below and answer the following TRUE or FALSE questions.

George Washington was the first president of the United States. He was born in 1732 and he died in 1799. He fought in the war against England from 1776 to 1781. This war was called the American Revolution. He became president in 1789, in New York.

There are many American cities named after George Washington. He is also on the one-dollar bill.

		True	False
1.	There is only one city named after George Washington.	❏	❏
2.	The American Revolutionary War was against England.	❏	❏
3.	George Washington's face appears on a $10 bill.	❏	❏
4.	The Revolutionary War ended after Washington became president.	❏	❏
5.	George Washington was the president of England.	❏	❏

0-1 ✖, enter date in chart on page 85 and go on to the next page; 2 or more ✖'s, go to Guidelines on page 87 and retest at a later date.

Main Idea

Read the following paragraph and answer the question that follows.

How to Draw a Straight Line

Straight lines are hard to draw. Sometimes they go up on the end and sometimes they go down. Sometimes they go all over the place. To make a line straight, try using something that has a smooth edge. Lay it down on the paper and run a pencil along the side of it. Almost any smooth edge may be used, like the edge of a book, the smooth side of a comb, or even a coat hanger. As long as you hold it down while you are drawing, it will give you a straight line.

The main idea is:

❑   Anything smooth and straight can be used to make a straight line.

❑   Some lines go up on the end.

❑   Use a coat hanger to make a straight line.

Reading	❑ fluent	❑ halting
Speed	❑ less than 1 minute	❑ more than 1 minute
Vocabulary	❑ 0-3 unknown words	❑ 3+ unknown words
Response	❑ correct	❑ incorrect

Correct response, enter date in chart on page 85 and go to the next page; incorrect response go to Guidelines on page 87 and retest at a later date.

Conclusions
Third Grade

Read the following paragraph and answer the question that follows.

Brown Snakes in Guam

Guam is an island in the middle of the Pacific Ocean. About 150,000 people live there, but they are outnumbered by the brown tree snake. Forty years ago, there were no brown tree snakes in Guam at all. Today there are more than a million. Nobody knows where they came from or how to stop them from multiplying. They have killed and eaten thousands of birds. Many kinds of rare birds and one kind of bat are becoming extinct because of the brown snake.

Why are many kinds of rare birds becoming extinct in Guam?

- ❑ Because they are multiplying.
- ❑ Because they outnumber the brown tree snake.
- ❑ Because the brown snakes are eating them all.

Reading	❑ fluent	❑ halting
Speed	❑ less than 1 minute	❑ more than 1 minute
Vocabulary	❑ 0-3 unknown words	❑ 3+ unknown words
Response	❑ correct	❑ incorrect

Correct response, enter date in chart on page 85 and go to the next page; incorrect response go to Guidelines on page 87 and retest at a later date.

....

Context

Choose the words that best complete each sentence.

1. A whale is a mammal that _____ (a) through an opening in the top of its head. This opening is called a blowhole. It is similar to a nostril. Although whales can stay under _____(b) for long periods of time, they must eventually surface to breathe.

     (a) ❑ swims   ❑ sees   ❑ breathes
     (b) ❑ air   ❑ water   ❑ land

2. Hawaii is an island made up of three volcanic mountains in the Pacific _____(a). The only active _____ (b) in the United States, outside of Alaska, are found in Hawaii.

     (a) ❑ Ocean   ❑ Sea   ❑ Lake
     (b) ❑ volcanoes   ❑ mountains   ❑ islands

3. A diamond is a mineral. It is the hardest substance known. It is actually a form of carbon, just like coal! Coal is _____ (a), but _____ (b) are usually clear or transparent.

     (a) ❑ black   ❑ narrow   ❑ liquid
     (b) ❑ coal   ❑ gold   ❑ diamonds

4. The kangaroo is a hopping marsupial commonly found in Australia. _____(a) means it has a pouch to carry its babies. Kangaroos have powerful hind legs, short forelimbs, and long muscular tails. Male kangaroos are called boomers and females are _____ (b) flyers.

(a) ❑ Kangaroo   ❑ Marsupial   ❑ Pouch
(b) ❑ said   ❑ called   ❑ females

5. A fossil is the remains or imprints of plants or _____(a) preserved from prehistoric times. Fossils are found in rocks, coal, or amber. Fossils left by both vertebrate and _____ (b) animals are valuable to scientists who study prehistoric life.

(a) ❑ vehicles   ❑ animals   ❑ plants
(b) ❑ invertebrate   ❑ vertebrate   ❑ living

0-2 ✖'s, enter date in chart on page 85 and go on to the next page; 3 or more ✖'s, go to Guidelines on page 87 and retest at a later date.

Fact Finding

Fourth Grade

Read the following paragraphs and tell if each sentence is TRUE or FALSE.

The ear is an organ of hearing and balance. The human ear has three parts—outer, middle, and inner.

The outer ear is the part we can see. It includes the skin-covered cartilage called the auricle or pinna. The middle ear is separated from the outer ear by the eardrum. It has three small bones known as the hammer, anvil, and stirrup. They were given these names because of their individual shapes. The inner ear contains the sound-analyzing cells. It also contains semicircular canals that regulate balance and orientation.

	True	False
1. The only function of the ear is to hear.	❏	❏
2. The ear has three distinct parts.	❏	❏
3. The inner ear regulates balance.	❏	❏
4. The outer ear has a bone that resembles a hammer.	❏	❏
5. The eardrum separates the middle and inner ear.	❏	❏

0-1 ✖, enter date in chart on page 85 and go on to the next page; 2 or more ✖'s, go to Guidelines on page 87 and retest at a later date.

Main Idea

Fourth Grade

Read the following story and answer the question that follows.

Bobby grew up in New York. He had been born there 11 years earlier and all of his friends were from his neighborhood.

Now, Bobby sat next to his father as he drove the station wagon down the long highway. The engine was overheating, and they would have to stop soon to rest. In the back seat, Bobby's mother was holding the baby as they both slept.

Although the Burnett family had left New York only three days before, it seemed like forever to Bobby. The long, boring ride made his legs feel like logs. His empty stomach was growling and he had a headache. Dad winked at Bobby as they rode along. "There's no turning back now," he said. Bobby tried to smile back at his father.

The main idea is:

❑ Moving to a new home is hard.
❑ Bobby grew up in New York.
❑ Traveling is exciting.

Reading	❑ fluent	❑ halting
Speed	❑ less than 1 minute	❑ more than 1 minute
Vocabulary	❑ 0-3 unknown words	❑ 3+ unknown words
Response	❑ correct	❑ incorrect

Correct response, enter date in chart on page 85 and go to the next page; incorrect response go to Guidelines on page 87 and retest at a later date.

Conclusions

Read the following story and answer the question that follows.

Stacey moved around her grandmother's stockroom whirling in graceful pirouettes. Her grandmother was typing at a nearby desk. Stacey's hair spun as she danced around.

Just then, Stacey heard her father calling her. She stopped dancing and hurried over to the cash register in the small market. "Your grandmother and I need some help in here," her father said. "Bring the bananas in from the loading dock. Then start mopping the floor so we'll be ready to open." As Stacey started down the stairs, she heard her father say, "Mom, I just don't know what to do about that girl. She's too busy dreaming about becoming a ballerina."

In a kind, gentle voice, her grandmother said to Stacey, "You have a special talent. You're going to be a great dancer. Someday your father will see that. So don't give up your dream."

This story shows that:

❏ Families should always stay together.

❏ Parents and children don't always agree.

❏ Parents and children are exactly alike.

Reading	❏ fluent	❏ halting
Speed	❏ less than 1 minute	❏ more than 1 minute
Vocabulary	❏ 0-3 unknown words	❏ 3+ unknown words
Response	❏ correct	❏ incorrect

Correct response, enter date in chart on page 85 and go to the next page; incorrect response go to Guidelines on page 87 and retest at a later date.

Context   *Fifth Grade*

Choose the words that best complete the sentences.

1. From the 9th to the 11th century, Scandinavian
_____ (a) called Vikings raided the coasts of
Europe, giving the _____ (b) the name the "Viking
Age." They were the best shipbuilders and sailors in the
world, and they traveled as far as Greenland and
Baghdad!

    (a) ❑ poets   ❑ warriors   ❑ weapons
    (b) ❑ period   ❑ traveling   ❑ prominent

2. Wolfgang Amadeus Mozart was an Austrian com-
poser. His music combines beautiful sound with classical
grace and technical perfection. A prodigy, he began
_____ (a) before he was five years old. During his
lifetime, he wrote works in almost every conceivable
_____ (b) of music.

    (a) ❑ driving   ❑ composing   ❑ recognizing
    (b) ❑ category   ❑ discussion   ❑ balance

3. Egypt of old is known as the Ancient Empire of the
Nile and was the site of one of the earliest civilizations.
Egypt was united about 3,200 BC and _____ (a) by
pharaohs (kings). Mummification and the building of
stone monuments began in the third _____ (b) ,
under the rule of the sun-worshippers—the religion of
the upper classes.

    (a) ❑ set   ❑ united   ❑ ruled
    (b) ❑ dynasty   ❑ minute   ❑ pyramid

4. The body contains three different vessels to carry blood. Arteries convey the blood away from the heart. The largest _____ (a) is called the aorta. Veins return the blood to the heart and lungs. The smallest are _____ (b) vessels called capillaries.

(a) ❑ aorta   ❑ artery   ❑ blood
(b) ❑ heart   ❑ vein   ❑ microscopic

5. The violin is a stringed musical instrument. It has a wooden body with a slightly convex back and front. The front is _____ (a) by two f-shaped resonance holes. It is played by _____ (b) a horsehair bow across the strings.

(a) ❑ pierced   ❑ covered   ❑ played
(b) ❑ throwing   ❑ delaying   ❑ drawing

0-2 ✖'s, enter date in chart on page 85 and go on to the next page; 3 or more ✖'s, go to Guidelines on page 87 and retest at a later date.

Fact Finding   *Fifth Grade*

Read the paragraph below and answer the following TRUE or FALSE questions.

Amelia Earhart was an American aviator who lived from 1898 to 1937. In 1928, she became the first woman to cross the Atlantic by airplane, and in 1932, she was the first woman to make a solo flight across the Atlantic. She was the first person, man or woman, to fly alone from Honolulu to California.

In 1937, she attempted to fly around the world, but her plane disappeared on the flight somewhere between New Guinea and Howland Island. To this day, her fate remains a mystery.

		True	False
1.	Amelia Earhart's goal was to fly around the world.	❏	❏
2.	Amelia Earhart was the first person to fly alone across the Atlantic Ocean.	❏	❏
3.	Amelia Earhart's plane disappeared when she was 39.	❏	❏
4.	Amelia Earhart's fate remains a mystery.	❏	❏
5.	Amelia Earhart's plane was found in Honolulu.	❏	❏

0-1 ✖, enter date in chart on page 85 and go on to the next page; 2 or more ✖'s, go to Guidelines on page 87 and retest at a later date.

Main Idea   *Fifth Grade*

Read the following story and answer the question that follows.

Southern Expeditions

For centuries, little was known about what was considered a distant, dangerous, frozen wasteland. Antarctica was the last continent to be discovered and was not sighted until the early 1800s. Since that time, many explorers have sailed south to visit the ice-covered land. In those days, their expeditions were as famous as those of the first astronauts.

Even before the land was discovered, stories were told about it. Centuries before anyone actually saw the continent, the ancient Greeks had thought that there was a continent at the bottom of the world. Over the years, tales of the undiscovered land grew. Some of the world's greatest sailors tried to find it. In 1772, the famous Captain James Cook undertook a grueling southern expedition.

Captain Cook was the first sailor to make it all the way to the ice cap that surrounds Antarctica in the winter. He sailed all the way around the continent but never actually saw it. Captain Cook went farther south than anyone had ever gone, and this record stood for 50 years.

In the 1820s, a different type of sailor was setting sail toward Antarctica—seal hunters and whale hunters such as a young American named

Palmer, who was probably the first person to see Antarctica. He and other adventurers were sailing through uncharted oceans in search of seals, and in doing so, became explorers as well as hunters. Nathaniel Palmer is believed to be the first person to see Antarctica.

The main idea is:

❑ Antarctica was not sighted until the early 1800s.

❑ Antarctica has been a source of fascination and intrigue for explorers for many centuries.

❑ Antarctica was the last continent to be discovered.

Reading	❑ fluent	❑ halting
Speed	❑ less than 1 minute	❑ more than 1 minute
Vocabulary	❑ 0-3 unknown words	❑ 3+ unknown words
Response	❑ correct	❑ incorrect

Correct response, enter date in chart on page 85 and go to the next page; incorrect response go to Guidelines on page 87 and retest at a later date.

Conclusions

Read the following story and answer the question that follows.

Seals

Seals are not fish. They're amphibious mammals that live both on the land and in the ocean. Some seals can stay at sea for months at a stretch—even sleeping in the water—but all seals need the land at some point. In order to avoid humans and other animals, they choose unpopulated areas to come onto the land.

Seals belong to a group of animals called "pinnipeds," or fin-footed, which includes the walrus, the sea lion, and the eared seal. Because of their fins, seals are excellent swimmers and divers. They have muscles in their noses that close their nostrils tightly when they dive. It is not unusual for them stay under water for as long as 30 minutes.

Being mammals, seals are warm-blooded animals that can adjust their bodies to various outside temperatures. They live in both warm and cold climates. Besides their fur, seals have a thick layer of fat called "blubber," which helps protect them against the cold. Unlike people, it is harder for seals to cool themselves off in hot weather and they can become ill or die if they get warm.

Answer the following questions about seals:

How Well Does Your Child Read?

1. Based on the other words in the sentence, what is the correct definition for "*amphibious*"?
   - ❑ living on the land
   - ❑ living on land and in the sea
   - ❑ living in large groups

2. Based on the other words in the sentence, what is the correct definition for "*pinniped*"?
   - ❑ smart
   - ❑ excellent swimmer
   - ❑ fin-footed

3. Based on the other words in the sentence, what is the correct definition for "*mammal*"?
   - ❑ warm-blooded animal
   - ❑ cold-blooded animal
   - ❑ warm-blooded fish

4. Based on the other words in the sentence, what is the correct definition for "*blubber*"?
   - ❑ fur
   - ❑ fat
   - ❑ layer of skin

5. Based on what you've read, where do seals live?
   - ❑ tropical climates
   - ❑ cold climates
   - ❑ dry climates

Reading	❑ fluent	❑ halting
Speed	❑ less than 1 minute	❑ more than 1 minute
Vocabulary	❑ 0-3 unknown words	❑ 3+ unknown words
Response	❑ correct	❑ 2+ incorrect

0-1 ✖, enter date in chart on page 85 and go to the next page; 2 or more ✖'s, go to Guidelines on page 87 and retest at a later date.

Reading Record

Use this chart to keep a record of your child's reading progress. Once your child has successfully completed an assessment, enter the date in the chart. This will enable you to track your child's reading skills development as well as the pace at which he is making progress. If your child does not successfully complete a particular assessment, you may want to use the reassessment for that grade level and skill. See page 141 for reassessments for kindergarten through 5th grade.

Date Passed	Skill	Level
	Matching Pictures	Kindergarten
	Matching Letters	
	Context	
	Fact Finding	
	Story Order	
	Story Sense	
	Context	1st Grade
	Fact Finding	
	Main Idea	
	Conclusions	

Reading Record—*continued*

Date Passed	Skill	Level
	Context	2nd Grade
	Fact Finding	
	Main Idea	
	Conclusions	
	Context	3rd Grade
	Fact Finding	
	Main Idea	
	Conclusions	
	Context	4th Grade
	Fact Finding	
	Main Idea	
	Conclusion	
	Context	5th Grade
	Fact Finding	
	Main Idea	
	Conclusions	

Grade Level Guidelines

The first things a parent with a beginning reader wants to know are: Where do we start? What comes first? What is important?

One of the main problems with parents teaching reading is not that they don't know enough, but that they *know too much*. It's hard to go all the way back to the very beginning.

Starting Point

For children, reading encompasses learning the alphabet, putting all the letters in the right order, printing them neatly and correctly, sounding them out and understanding the meaning. For them, it's like trying to see the forest for the trees. Each element may be clear, but putting them all together for the big picture is extremely difficult. Parents on the other hand are generally literate, but have forgotten all the bits and pieces that go into the process of reading.

Fortunately, there is a comfortable sequence that enables children to learn phonics, and leads naturally into reading.

In terms of working with your own child, however, it is crucial to remember that there are stages of learning, types of memory, ways of learning, and internal time frames in which children learn. In general, children learn by doing. They are more successful with hands-on, concrete exercises, rather than more abstract, bookish exercises. For example, having your child rearrange letter cards to form a word will make a stronger, longer-lasting impression than if he just sits and looks at words on a page.

Some children are adroit psychological game players. They may pretend to forget large amounts of information, (*What? I didn't know that, really!*). If you feel yourself getting upset (*But you **know** this word!* or *We've been **over** this!* or *Are you paying attention?*), it's time to back off and make a fresh start later.

Reading is an enjoyable activity, not a punishment, and it should be taught playfully and lovingly. One day, reading will all make sense for your child. Your job, as a parent, is to keep practicing the fundamentals until that day comes.

Reading should be fun, not work

There will be a wide range in ability, interest, and performance among children at the beginning stages of reading. It may extend from an engaged interest to complete detachment and disinterest in books and reading. Almost all children, however, love to be read *to*. Don't be alarmed if at this early stage your child makes no connection between the spoken word and the printed word. This is natural because reading is a complex concept that takes time to be learned.

By reading to your child you will help him pick up the pre-basics: holding the book, turning the pages one at a time in the right direction, and following the pictures in a logical order. In time, with gentle encouragement, he will start to make the tenuous connection between letters printed on the page and actual spoken sounds, words, and ideas.

Reading *is* serious, but children need to be taught playfully. Two games that work well are variations on old standards—*Concentration* and *Go Fish*. For *Concentration*, start by using cards with matching pictures, then make cards with pictures that rhyme. Move on to cards with letters, rhyming words, and so on. In regular *Go Fish*, you use cards with numbers and players ask, for example, "Do you have a six?" In *Go Phish* (the phonics version), you use cards with letters or, later on, words. Players ask "Do you have a *T*?" or "Do you have a *Dog*?"

Books versus TV

There is a strong correlation between watching too much television and weak literacy. There is also a strong correlation between how much a family reads and the overall literacy of its members. The earlier you start reading to your child, the better, but it's never too late to pick up the habit. Read bedtime stories, take books along in the car—the parent not driving or an older sibling can read aloud, or the child can read on his own. This is a perfect setting for presenting your child with the idea of reading for fun, because generally there are no distractions from video games, television, and other attractions.

Take your child to the library to check out books of his choice and find out what programs your town's public library might have to encourage children to read.

Mostly, model the behavior your want your child to follow. Let your child see you reading and, when appropriate, talk to him about what you've read.

If you find it difficult to change your family's television viewing vs. reading habits, try a no-TV week for the entire household. This will be a great way for your child (and you) to discover the pleasure of reading.

Reading Prep

Spontaneous reading can and should happen any-where—while waiting in the car, at the doctor's office, in the park. However, it's good for your child to have a comfortable routine for reading. Here are some guidelines:

1. Find a quiet place for you and your child to read together uninterrupted for at least 10 minutes at a time.

2. Sit next to your child, so he can follow along with the words as you read.

3. Show your child the first page and how to open a book correctly.

4. Occasionally indicate words or phrases by pointing to them and moving your finger in a left to right direction as you read. For example, say, *"Oh, look, here's where it tells what the little bear said."* Indicate with your finger and follow the words as you read. *"My porridge is all gone! Someone has eaten all my porridge!"*

5. Review the story plot following the reading. Say, *"What did the little bear do when his chair was broken? What happened next?"* Three to four questions per story is enough.

6. When your child is familiar with the story, have him "read" it to you, using picture clues, while holding the book on his own lap.

7. As your child learns his letter names and sounds, show him selected words while reading. Say, *"See this word, it starts with the same letter 'b' as your name, Bobby. Can you find a letter in this line that says 'sss'?"*

Memorizing Words

In order to get a word firmly in your child's memory, it is helpful for him to really focus on it with the following sequence. This technique is not just for beginning readers. It can be used through college for memorizing new vocabulary, scientific terms, mathematical formulas, or foreign language vocabulary.

1. *Look* at the word.
2. *Say* the word.
3. *Cover* the word.
4. *Remember* what the word looks like.
5. *Write* the word from memory.
6. *Check* the word. Uncover it and check each letter carefully.

Reading is a habit, and it is your job as a parent to make sure that your child picks up this lifelong habit at an early age. Make books and other reading materials a part of your daily life. Have age-appropriate dictionaries handy for when a new word comes up. Mention items of interest in the newspaper. Point out that the television guide doesn't count as literature. Don't forget that habits have to be reinforced. As soon as your child can read on his own, set aside 10 minutes for daily reading. As he gets older, increase the time—15 minutes in 2nd grade, 20 minutes in 3rd grade, and so on. By the time your child is in 5th grade, he should feel comfortable choosing, reading, and using books on a wide range of topics and on a regular basis.

Following are the grade level guidelines for kindergarten through 5th grade, with the basic topics and common difficulties for each grade.

Phonics Definitions

Vowels. A, E, I, O, U and sometimes Y and W. Every word and syllable must have at least one vowel.

Consonants. Remaining letters and usually Y and W.

Consonant blends. Two or more *consonants* sounded together in such a way that *each* is heard—*black, train, cry, swim, fling.*

Consonant digraphs. Two *consonants* that together represent *one sound—when, thin, this, church, sheep, know, write, pack, thing.*

Consonant clusters. Three *consonants* that together represent *one sound—street, scrap, spring.*

Vowel digraphs. Two *vowels* that together represent *one sound,* for example, *school, book, bread, auto, yawn, eight.* Normally, with a double vowel, the first vowel stands for a long sound and the second is silent (*rain, jeep, heat, soap)* or the two vowels make a double sound—a diphthong (*coin or house).* With vowel digraphs, however, these rules are not followed.

Sight word. A word that does not follow the basic rules of spelling, and cannot be sounded out. For example, *pet* and *Pete* follow the rules, whereas *laughed* is pronounced *laft.* Sight words just need to be memorized or learned—by sight.

Syllable. A unit consisting of one vowel sound, with a consonant placed before or behind it. If you hear only one vowel sound in a word (*joke, miles*), it's a one-syllable word and cannot be divided. If you hear two vowel sounds (*basket, people*), it's a two-syllable word.

Kindergarten

Basic Skills

Most kindergartners should know how to say or sing the alphabet. They should be able to recognize their own names in print. Some may know how to print the alphabet, both upper and lower case, but this depends on their fine motor skills. They should know the positions—right, left, top, and bottom. This will help them know how to put their name on their papers in the proper position, how to follow the text from left to right and top to bottom, and how to open the book at the front, rather than the back. They need to know that there are *letters* in the alphabet and the association between each letter and its sound. They should also know that when you put the sounds together, they make *words*.

In texts appropriate for kindergartners, there should be a picture for every sentence, so that they can *see* the idea and then back it up with words.

Adults tend to take for granted that a story has a particular order, probably chronological. Children need to have this reinforced. You can do this by using daily examples such as putting on shoes and socks. Ask your child questions like, *"Which do you put on first? Why?"* She will naturally know the answer. But, having to stop, think about it and explain it will help develop logic sequencing. As a parent and adult, you have to remember that concepts that you take for granted need to be pointed out to your child, using concrete examples.

Story order exercises help a child see a story develop and, at the same time, tell stories himself. This storytelling precedes the written word and will get your child thinking in a certain way.

Furthermore, children need to have logical consequences pointed out and reinforced. Discuss how the first picture leads into the second one, and then have your child choose the logical third and explain why this choice makes sense. A kindergartner should be able to finish a story in a logical way, as well as predict the outcome.

Kindergartners are now ready for *Go Fish* and *Concentration* games with easy words, such as *cat, pet,* and *dog*.

Another way to develop your child's readiness for reading is to have her make flash cards. Participation will encourage your child to use the cards, and the actual writing will be a memory aid.

Common Difficulties

At each age and at each stage there are particular trouble spots that show up:

1. **Awareness of the Alphabet.**
    When a pre-reader starts to understand that there is a relationship between those little marks on a page and the sounds that come out of our mouths, she is on her way to reading. This is a highly abstract concept for a 5-year-old, but the sooner you start with an awareness of the alphabet, the longer your child will have to internalize the 26 symbols and the sounds they represent.

2. **Name and Sound of the Letter.**
    Another level of difficulty in the English alphabet is that there is a difference between the "name" of the letter and the "sound" of the

letter. For example, the name of the letter *S* is *ess*, but the sound of the letter is *sss*. This is an important distinction for your child to make, because it helps immediately with sounding out short words. Later on, it is used to clarify long and short vowels and to distinguish between hard and soft consonants (*C* as in *cat* or as in *nice*).

3. **Similar Letter Shapes.**

It is common to see children confused by the *four corners* letters:

b	d
p	q

One solution is to choose the key letter—*b*—and make sure that your child understands it. Use several approaches. Trace the *b* on your child's back and say *bee*. Take a <u>b</u>asketball and a <u>b</u>at and use them to form the letter *b*. She can see the spatial relationship of the ball and the bat, so the ball is where the *loop* goes and the bat is the *stick*. Talk about the ball being on the right side and the bat being on the left. Move the ball and have your child put the ball to the right of the bat. Then have her copy the pattern by writing *b*'s on paper.

Once she solidly knows **b**, she can go on to **d**, then **p** and finally **q**.

Another approach is that **d** and **q** are really the same as **a**, but **d** has a taller stick going up, and **q** has a tail going down.

4. **Socialization and Manners.**
   In addition to these concrete methods that
   you can use to help your child learn the
   alphabet, there are also some more intangible
   ways that are equally important. The
   presence or absence of a child's social skills
   will be a large factor in the ease or difficulty
   with which she succeeds. According to the
   U.S. Department of Education, "The single
   best childhood predictor of adult adaptation is
   not IQ, *not* school grades, and *not* classroom
   behavior, but rather the adequacy with which
   the child gets along with other children."
   (Hartup, 1992) Children need to go to school
   prepared to get along with others, share
   books and toys, and take turns playing,
   listening, and helping.

More Kindergarten Skills

Letter Patterns. Recognizing *letter patterns* is very
important for developing the pre-reading skills. Have
your child find and circle the same letter groups from a
list of similar ones. For example:

To give your child a grasp of a word (c-u-p, for example), use exercises that give the first and last consonant, and have your child fill in the blank with one of

the suggested vowels. Make sure that you use pictures and that you say the word repeatedly, both as a word *(cup),* and as individual sounds *(kuh-uh-puh).* It is very important to keep the "uh" part of "kuh" or "puh" almost silent. Your goal is only the consonant sound. An over-pronounced "uh" will lead to difficulties with syllables later on.

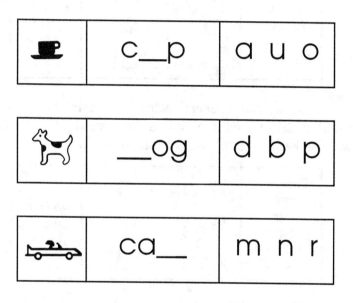

Hint: When you are helping a kindergartner with this type of exercise, cover up everything except the row you are working on. The whole exercise may look too "busy" to a child's eye.

Word Families. Play with rhyming word cards and point out the tiny differences that change the sound of the word—for example, by changing just one letter the word *cat* becomes *mat,* then *hat,* and so on. The example shown below should give you a good start at this. Rearranging the cards and saying the words provide visual, tactile, and auditory reinforcement. Remember that each of these "modalities" is good, but exercises that combine two or three are much more effective.

These are minimal changes— just the first letter.	c r s	at at at	*at* is the word family.

Use this type of exercise to show your child how a different letter sound makes a new word. Repeat this exercise with letter changes at the end of a word:

These are more minimal changes— just the last letter.	ma ma ma	n t d	*ma* is the word family.

and in the middle of a word:

These are still more minimal changes— just the middle letter.	c c c	a u o	p p p

First Grade

Basic Skills

Children learn to sound out words and begin basic reading in the 1st grade. The basic rules of phonics from the alphabet to long vowels are learned at this age. First graders should be able to read age-appropriate texts, sound out words they haven't seen before, and figure out simple meanings from the context.

By the end of 1st grade, children should be able to identify the *syllables* in a word, using them to distinguish between the base word and the various endings (log, logs, logged, logger, logging).

Also, by the end of the year, students should be familiar with the *mechanics* of reading—the rules of pronunciation (including consonants, consonant blends, short vowels, and long vowels), and the lists of sight words and high frequency words.

It is not unusual to see a child still reversing words and letters at this stage—*d* for *b* and *no* for *on*, etc. This is not a cause for worry or a panic about dyslexia. If you suspect, however, that there is an actual reading problem, do not hesitate to discuss this with the school principal or the eye doctor. There are educational measures that can be taken to ease the way for a child with reading or vision difficulties.

Children will also track their reading with their fingers at this age. This is not an impediment. The eye muscles have not yet developed sufficiently to track back and forth, and the comprehension level is not high enough to keep place without a physical marker.

Moving on from the actual mechanics of reading, 1st graders should be able to say what the main point or main idea of a story is, in general terms. Furthermore, they should draw simple conclusions and explain why certain characters behaved the way they did. They should also have opinions about what happened in a story.

In terms of reading aloud, encourage your 1st grader to start using punctuation as a guide to how sentences sound. A statement—ending in a period—should sound different from a question—ending in a question mark.

When you and your child are reading, you will often be asked about a word—its meaning, pronunciation, why it is spelled a certain way. This is an excellent habit to encourage. Immediately say the word back to him. If a child can see a word and then hear it immediately after, it will reinforce the connection between print and sound. When he makes a mistake, don't make a big deal about it; mistakes are a natural part of life.

When a child can figure a word out from the context, he is really starting to read. He is putting all the pieces together—phonics, vocabulary, and comprehension. In order to help with this, read the same books over and over, pausing at his favorite spots, so he can fill in the gaps. For a 5- or 6-year-old, it is quite common to memorize a whole story without being able to read yet. There are many benefits to this. He learns how to tell a story, what the rhythms and patterns of the language are, and new vocabulary in the story. By repetition and pictures, he is able to make sense of it. Later, as he comes to understand the sound-letter relationship, the underlying structure will support his learning.

Once children have a good grasp of one-syllable words, they can use that same skill to move on to longer words. Being able to find the small word within a big word is a great advantage to an early reader. For example, *fantastic* is a *big* word to a 1st grader, but *fan* can be sounded out, as can *tas* and *tic*. When they put them all together as *fan•tas•tic*, they've sounded out a big word.

Reading and Being Read to

It is generally accepted wisdom that reading to a child will help produce a reader. The more you read aloud to your child, the more familiar he will be with the idea of books, the idea of getting pleasure and information from books, the recognition of letters on the printed page, and the correlation of printed words and information.

However, a child's reading skills will lag far behind his spoken language abilities for the first six to 10 years of his life. Talking and listening are effortless, but reading and writing take work. So, a child who is used to listening to advanced books may become bored and frustrated when he is only able to read a beginning book.

Other children, to the despair of their parents, will just read the same "baby books" over and over again. This gives a child an immediate sense of success. It gives him the idea that *"I can read."* Through the 1st grade, rereading familiar material reinforces the basics of reading, trains the eye coordination for consistent reading, satisfies the child's needs for the familiar and the comfortable, and allows the child himself to figure out new word based on their context.

Parents are well aware of the importance of reading and the enormous effect it will have on their child's future. Every parent wants his or her child to read, to read well, and to read often. There are not many guarantees in life, but if you sit patiently with your child night after night and read interesting stories, explain the rules of reading, reinforce this understanding with his own reading, and finally, read a lot yourself, you will have a child who reads. Naturally, there will be voracious readers, who devour every printed surface in the house and there will be more informational readers, who read to get what they want. But if you go through the steps, you will achieve 100 percent literacy in your home.

Common Difficulties

For each grade level, there are certain challenges that arise. In 1st grade, the following are common.

1. **Confusion between *long* and *short* vowels.**
   While a 1st grader should know the short vowels (*bat, bet, bit, hot, but*), he may not distinguish between *mat* and *mate*. You might hear the second word read as *mat*, *matee, ma-teh*. Explain the *silent E* rule, and that E "has a job to do." The final E makes the vowel say its name, but the E itself is completely silent. Similarly, when they are in the early writing stages, they may just put the first letter (I l t p → I like to play) or write the consonants, leaving the vowels out (picture → pkchr).

2. **Different learning styles.**
   Some children wiggle around and concentrate less, while others sit more quietly and grasp concepts more quickly. But there is more than one way of learning. It is important to use all of the senses in order to find the ones that work for the particular student: Visual (*shapes*), auditory (*sounds*), kinesthetic (*touching* and *feeling*).

3. **Frustration with exceptions.**
   Once a child has mastered a rule, exceptions to the rule can be intensely frustrating. Explain that some words don't follow the rules and that they can't be sounded out.

4. **Understanding the *phonics*, but not integrating them into *reading*.**
   It's a big leap to go from looking at letters on a page to making them tell a story. If a child gets stuck on a word, you can fill in the blanks for him. If you notice a pattern of missing words, it could be a gap in understanding of the rules. It helps to have your child say the rule back to you.

5. **Forgetting words they "knew" well.**
   Kids learn in stages. Sometimes something committed to short-term memory will just slip out the back door. Relax and go over it again. Don't get frustrated or your child will shut down and be afraid to try.

6. **Leaving the word out.**
   Some children simply skip over words they don't know. If your child skips a word, backtrack and repeat the entire phrase. This puts the word in context for him, letting him hear the flow of the entire sentence with the word in place.

7. **Mumbling difficult words.**
   Language is originally and primarily an oral communication system. Often, when a child is telling a story, he can mumble a detail he's not quite sure of and keep going, as long as it doesn't break the rhythm of the story. In

reading, too, difficult words will be mumbled over. If this happens too frequently, the entire meaning can be lost. Children get nervous reading, and not knowing a word can be embarrassing. Clarify the pronunciation for your child. If it follows a phonetic rule, have your child sound it out. If it is a sight word, quickly explain both the pronunciation and meaning. Try not to disrupt the flow of the reading. Also, a child can sound loud in his own head, not realizing how quietly the words are coming out. Try telling him to "shout" it out once or twice so he can feel what louder speech sounds like.

8. **Making up words.**
   Frequently younger children will just look at the first letter and say a word that starts with that same letter. Of course, all meaning is lost. If this happens, ask if the sentence makes sense with the words used. Have him reread it slowly, sounding out the words. Talk about the meaning of the sentence in particular and the story in general.

9. **Over-pronouncing the T.**
   At some point, readers will come up against a quirk of American English, which is that *T* and *D* sound the same, as in *latter* and *ladder*. In reading, encourage them to make the leap from the over-pronounced *let-ter* to the word that they know and use, *letter*. Also, the *T* at the end of a word is hardly pronounced in speech. But is highly visible, so children get confused and want to put a big *T* sound at the end of a word.

10. **Getting stuck on the first letter and stopping.**
Because the first letter, generally a consonant, is introduced early and often to the new reader, it seems children can get stuck there. They will look at a word such as *car*, and say k-k-k-k-, without going on the next sound. Or, if they do go on, they get confused and stop making sense. Ask what word would make *sense* at that point. For example, if the sentence is *The bear is walking in the woods* and the child is having trouble with the word *woods*, talk about bears, where they live, and what that particular bear might be doing.

More First Grade Skills

As your child is learning to read and grasp the concepts of phonics and how letters make words, here are guidelines to help your child learn to read.

1. Pay close attention to the **order in which you introduce the letters** and **how you relate each letter to its sound**. Keep it simple. Too much information is overwhelming. For example, the letter A has six different pronunciations, but a beginning reader should only learn the short A of *cat*.*

2. Children should practice **reading to themselves** rather than reading out loud. The reason for this is to develop the eye coordination to track side to side and line to

line, as children read more quickly to themselves than they can out loud.

3. Focus on **upper case letters** in the beginning, then move to lower case. In kindergarten and early 1st grade, most children use all capital letters to write words, including their names. In 1st grade, children learn to distinguish between the two cases and to use them appropriately. Do *not* introduce them at the same time (i.e. **A a**).

4. Practice sounding out words that **follow the rules**, such as *cat*, *late*, etc.

5. Words that can't be sounded out should be learned as **sight words**, such as *laugh, mother, have*, etc.

6. Whenever your child sounds a word out, make sure that he knows the **meaning**.

7. Fairly advanced words such as *Christmas* or *Reebok* might be absorbed as sight words early on, due to the great exposure to them that children experience.

8. When the beginning reader is first learning to sound words out, practice **word families** *(bat, cat, sat, mat, hat)*. Point out that only the first letter changes, and that all the words rhyme.

9. Let your child **track the words** across the page with his finger, or have him use an index card to keep each line separate. Immature eyes will "stand" on each word, and not flow over to the next words on a line. Additionally, it is very easy for a child to lose

track from line to line. A card or ruler to guide the eye will help.

10. Have your child write as well as read, (a daily journal, the shopping list, letters, etc.).

*The Six 'A' Sounds: *pack, pace, park, final, parent, war.*

High-Frequency Words. Not all words are used equally. Researchers have actually counted which words are used most, and consequently, *should be known best by students*. Here are the first 100 of those words. The other 400 are in Appendix 4 on page 187. Have your child practice flying through these words. Use flashcards. And, of course, use Dr. Seuss. This way, your child can practice these common function words, both in and out of context. Generally speaking, their recognition and reading will be better in context.

The First 100

the	of	and	a	to	in	is
you	that	it	he	for	was	on
are	as	with	his	they	at	be
this	from	I	have	or	by	one
had	not	but	what	all	where	
when	we	there	can	an	your	
their	said	if	do	will	each	
about	how	up	no	out	them	
then	she	many	some	so	these	
would	other	into	has	more	her	
two	like	him	see	time	could	
make	than	first	been	its	who	
now	people	my	made	over	did	
down	only	way	find	use	may	
after	long	little	very	after	words	
called	just	where	most	know	which	

Consonant Blends. Blends don't seem like they should be difficult, but they often are hard for children to put together. This is because they learn the individual consonants first (B *buh* and L *luh*), so when they try to form even a simple word such as *blue*, it comes out as *buh-luh-oo*. It only gets more complicated with **clusters**, with *suh-tuh-er-eet* instead of *street*.

At this point, you have to get your child to make the connection between words that he already knows and the sounds that he's trying to create from the printed page. He can say *street*, so that's half the battle. Work on isolating the sound, *str*, and practice saying it out loud. *Street, str, str-eet, str, street.* Then, go back to the printed word, cover up the back end, and correlate the sound and the letters. Once the spoken *str* matches the written one, uncover the back end and let the whole word come out, *street*.

Word Endings. It takes time for a child to realize that a word can have parts to it. He might think *walked* looks like a two-syllable word (*wal-ked*) and not be able to figure it out. But when he understands that it is *walk* plus an *-ed* ending, reading becomes easier.

When your child has trouble with one of these words, cover up the ending, so the child can read the easy part (a word he may already be familiar with), then uncover the suffix and let him add it on (for the big word). His grammar skills will take over, and he will say *walk̲e̲d̲* instead of *wal-ked*, and later will know to spell it as *walked* instead of *walkt*.

Spelling and Pronunciation. In the 1st grade, children learn to spell according to certain rules. Spelling changes in order to maintain pronunciation. In a nutshell, the main rules are:

1. The *e* reaches over and makes the vowel say its name.
   rat → *rate*   *not* → *note*   *fin* → *fine*

2. When two vowels go a-walking,
   The first one does the talking.
   bed → *bead*   *got* → *goat*   *ran* → *rain*

Adding an ending (*ing, ed, er, est*) can cause changes. The rules are:

1. For short vowels, double the consonant.
   hop →   *hopping   hopped   hopper*

2. Long vowels lose the silent *e* and keep the single consonant.
   hope →   *hoping   hoped   hoper*

Even with the rules introduced, there will be vestigial phonetic sounding out. Your child may write things that sound like they should be there, but really aren't, such as *gowing* for *going*. To remedy this, review the ending with other words (*ask+**ing**, show+**ing***) so the child can see and understand the pattern.

Reading is made up of several discrete skills. Two of the most distinct are reading and spelling. Good readers are not necessarily good spellers, and some excellent spellers never pick up a book. To illustrate this, if you read the imaginary word *feen*, there is only one way to pronounce it. However, if you are asked to spell a word that sounds like *feen*, you could come up with *feen, fene, fean*, or *phean*. This is because there are different spelling rules that can apply to the long E sound as well as the F sound. If a child knows the spelling rules, reading will be easy. Spelling words still need to be addressed on a case by case basis.

More Spelling Rules. Here are a few rules that will help your child with spelling and pronunciation.

Short Vowel Rule: If a word or syllable has only one vowel and it comes at the beginning or between two consonants, the vowel usually stands for a short sound— *am, is, bag, fox.*

Long Vowel Rule 1: Silent *e* rule. If a one-syllable word ends in an E, the vowel is long—*make, time, more, Pete, rule.*

Long Vowel Rule 2: Two vowels walking rule. If a one-part word or syllable has two vowels, the first vowel usually stands for a long sound and the second is silent—*rain, jeep, heat, soap.*

Long Vowel Rule 3: Final vowel rule. If a word or syllable has one vowel and it comes at the end of the word or syllable, the vowel usually stands for a long sound. For example: *we, go, cupid, pony.*

***Y* as a Vowel Rules.** If Y is the only vowel at the end of a one-syllable word, Y sounds like long I: *fly, try, by.* If Y is the only vowel at the end of a word of more than one syllable, Y usually has a sound like: *silly, funny, baby.*

Soft *C* and *G* Rule. When C or G are followed by E, I, or Y, a soft sound is produced: *ice, city, range, gym.*

Double Vowels. One of the most difficult areas for young children is the wide variety in vowel combinations and the subsequent pronunciation. There are both regular and irregular double vowels. The boxed words follow Long Vowel Rule 2, but the rest are exceptions. This aspect of reading, sight words, just requires *practice.*

ou	house, mouse, douse, louse

but   soup, four, touch, through, though, rough, cough, courage, furious

ea	seat, meat, treat, neat

but   head *or* hear *or* heard *or* heart *or* great *or* idea *or* create *or* beautiful *or* theatre *or* theatrical *or* bureau

ow	how, now, brown, cow

but   show, low, throw

ie	tried, lied, fried

but   friend *or* fiend *or* diet *or* deity *or* icier *or* orient *or* derriere

oa	soap, boat, toast, goat

but   broad

oo	tooth, booth, choose, loose

but   took, good, look

The regular double vowels are EA, EE, AI, OA, IE, AY and OW. Irregular double vowels are very difficult for new readers because there are so many exceptions. Even adults have to check back in certain circumstances. Remember this old poem?

Have You Heard the Word?

Beware of *heard*, a dreadful *word*,
That looks like *beard* and sounds like *bird*,
And *dead*: It's said like *bed* not *bead* —
For goodness sakes, don't call it *deed*.
Watch out for *meat* and *great* and *threat*,
(They rhyme with *suite* and *straight* and *debt*.)

Believe it or not, irregular words are in the minority in terms of the words in the English language. More than 80 percent of the words in the dictionary are regular—but the problem is that in everyday language, we don't use the dictionary words. We use common terms that we've worn down and gotten used to over the centuries. These have come out to be irregular though this daily use.

The good news is that once the new reader gets past the familiar, but highly irregular words of colloquial speech, he will find that the longer, more sophisticated, Latin- and Greek-based words of literature will seem simple by comparison and simple to sound out.

R-Controlled Vowels. An R-controlled vowel means that an R can change the pronunciation of the previous vowel—the short *o* of *hot* turns into the long *o* of *horn*. It helps to remember two of the early sight words *or* and *for* have a long *o*. Another tricky thing about R is that sometimes the vowel in front of it is pronounced, *here*, and sometimes it isn't, *her*.

Children first learn *R* as a single consonant—*run* or *red*. Later, *R* is incorporated into a blend or cluster—*trip* or *shrill*. Next, they learn the *-er* ending—*runner* or *later*. And finally, there are the R-controlled vowels—*more*, *care* or *fire*.

Vowel Combo	Basic Rule	Final *E* Rule	Silent Vowel Before *R*	Sight Words
ar	car	care	dollar	arrive
ir	spirit	fire	first	siren
er	very	here	herd	her
or	for	more	color	word
ur	fur	cure	fur	bury

The problem with the consonant *R* and the R-controlled vowels is that they are two different *R*'s. The consonant *R* is regular whereas R-controlled vowels are not. When a child first comes across a word like *faster*, he may read it as *fast•air* or *fast•eer* and spell it as *fastr*. The word *first* may be read as *feerst* or *fyrst,* and spelled as *frst*. This situation necessitates the introduction of the *-er* ending. Once they have *-er* drilled into them, however, it can become the only option, with *ferst, hert, werst,* and *coler* showing up in spelling before *feerst* disappears from reading.

It helps to pare down the options. Primarily, *-er* is an ending. It is not common in the beginning of a word, except for *where*, *here* and *there*. Fortunately, *-ar* and *-or* are clearly pronounced, so for an R-controlled vowel, the real distinction is between *-ir* and *-ur*, as in *fir* and *fur*.

L-Controlled Vowels. An L-controlled vowel means that an L can change the pronunciation of the previous vowel. There are a couple of little things to help an early reader. First, '*ol*' has a long *o*. It's easy for 1st graders to remember by starting with the word *old* and building up from there. You ask the child, *"Can you find the little word in the big word?"* Whenever you have an -*old* base, cover up the first letter so your child can read *old*, then move your finger and he can add on. ***c*** + *old*, ***g*** + *old*, ***t*** + *old*. *Colt* and *bolt* can coattail on this.

-*old*	told, fold, hold, bold, sold, cold, gold, mold
-*all*	cal, tall, stall, hall, ball, fall, wall
-*oll*	doll, follow
-*alk*	talk, walk, chalk
-*ald*	cold, bolt, bald, scald

Call may be read as *cal* for a while, but since *all* is learned early, use the same technique. ***c*** + *all*, ***b*** + *all*, ***t*** + *all*. *Bald* can coattail, but *walk* and *talk* are sight words (with a silent L!).

Soft Consonants. Children learn early that vowels have different pronunciations, but they generally learn consonants as having a single sound. At this stage, they need to learn that when a *C* is followed by *a, o,* or *u,* the letter *c* usually sounds like *k*. But when it is followed by an *e* or an *i*, it takes the soft *s* sound.

Hard C = K

ca-	cat, call, catch, can, cave, car
co-	come, copy, cough, cost
cu-	cut, customer, cub, cup

Soft C = S

ci-	city, circus, circuit, cinnamon
ce-	certain, center, celebrate, certificate
ice	nice, police, Janice, lattice
uce	truce, lettuce, spruce, deuce
ace	race, place, trace, face, lace
ece	piece, niece, fleece

Similarly, there are two *g* sounds. When *g* is followed by an *a*, *o* or *u*, it takes the hard *g* sound. *Gi* and *ge* can also sometimes be the hard *g*. When a *g* is followed by an *e*, it takes the soft *j* sound. There are a few exceptions such as *get*. Sometimes a *gi* or *gy* will sound like *j*.

Hard G = G

ga-	gas, gap, gave, gain, gallop
go-	go, gone, got, goat
gu-	gum, guppy, gullible, gustatory
ge-	get, gecko, gear, geyser
gi-	girl, gift

Soft G = J

ge-	gentle, George, general, gem
gi-	giant, ginger, giraffe, gin
gy-	gym, Gypsy, biology
age	cage, stage, garage, page
uge	huge, gauge, gouge, refuge

Hint: Sometimes E has two jobs. There is the old job of making the vowel say its name, and a new one of turning the *G* into *J*, or turning *C* into *S*.

That Tricky Y. Sometimes the letter Y sounds like a long I and sometimes like a long E. The trick is to remember an easy one-syllable word, like *my*, and then add on the correlated ones. Once that is secure, go on to the two-syllable words, making a big distinction for the different ending sound.

One Syllable = I
fly, fry, spy, try, my, shy, by, cry

Two Syllables = E
pretty, silly, funny, happy, party
any, many, penny, money, honey

I and Y are actually closely related, with Y being the Greek I, as they call it in French. You can see the transition from Y to I in *penny* to *penniless*, *lady* to *ladies*, *easy* to *easily*, etc.

Second Grade

Basic Skills

Second graders should have the basic reading skills. Sounding out should be second nature and the child should start reading in longer and longer phrases, rather than word by word.

Reading should consist of stories with fewer pictures than before, and the child should be able to follow a simple story line. Second graders start reading chapter books.

Every child should sit and read for at least 15 minutes a day. He can be with a parent or on his own, reading out loud or silently to himself. Choosing the book himself will give him greater incentive to read. Although the book may seem too easy to the parent, or it may be that he has read the book 900 times, let your child choose the book for the 15 minute reading. Your job is to make certain that the child sits still and reads. This means checking to make sure that his eyes are moving back and forth on the page. Encourage him to ask both how to pronounce a word and what it means.

After mastering phonics, the child starts working towards the *bigger picture* of reading. This raises the *point* of reading—is it to entertain oneself, to gather information, to integrate one's experience with that of the world, to understand a multicultural perspective? It is any or all of these, depending on the child, and his needs and motivations.

In order to arrive at any of these points, however, he will need to start using the following four tools. These are not limited to 2nd grade reading and there are more that will be introduced in the higher grades, but these will hold any reader in good stead through college and beyond. The earlier children learn these skills, and the more adroit they become at implementing them, the more satisfying their reading will be on a personal level, and the more effective their reading and writing will be on academic and professional levels.

Common Difficulties

1. **Main Idea.** This is *big-picture* understanding as opposed to noticing the *details*. This skill lets a child step back and think about the whole story. For a 2nd grader, the main idea is generally in the first sentence. The *main idea sentence* tells about the whole story, using all the details to add up to the entirety. A question that elicits main point understanding is, *"What is this story mostly about?"*

2. **Fantasy vs. Reality.** By the 2nd-grade stage, when a child is talking to someone, there is a fairly clear distinction between something that actually happened, and something that is imaginary, pretend, possible, or untrue. A large part of this understanding comes from the presentation of the information—an awareness of the real context, the speaker's attitude or tone of voice, etc. In reading, however, (as they are generally still at the monotone stage), they tend to miss some of the clues that would indicate whether something actually happened or not. In order to help the child distinguish, ask questions about what happened. Then, if you notice the child going astray, you can point

out the references that support either reality or fantasy. Ask, *"What would have happened if...?"* or *"Could he really fly?"* or *"How could...?"* Use starter questions to get your child thinking creatively, rather than answering questions about who did what to whom, and when.

3. **Drawing Conclusions.** In a story, the writer doesn't spell out every last detail—there are things that a reader will need to figure out or guess at. Conclusions are drawn from information given, (*He did it again!*—The word *again* allows the reader to conclude that something has happened before.) The type of question that enable a child to draw logical conclusions is *"What do you think would happen from that? Why?"* or *"What can you tell from the story?"* or *"From the story, what do you know about ...?"* or *"How do you think this person (character) would feel? Why?"*

   A good conclusion exercise is to give the child specific information and have him come up with the situation. For example, *"You see bats, balls and gloves. You hear, 'Strike One!' You smell hot dogs. Where are you?"*

4. **Getting the Facts.** When teachers ask the class to *get the facts* of a story, they are really looking for the details. The first thing a reader does is to get the main idea. Then, he goes on and finds the facts that support the main idea. The type of questions that elicit an awareness and understanding of the details might ask about what someone looked like, what they said or did, and when things happened. This is

where the journalistic 5 W's come into play,
and their correlating responses:

Who?	He. She. It.
What?	The tree.
Where?	Here. There. Everywhere.
When?	Yesterday, tomorrow, Monday.
Why?	Because...
How?	By doing...

More Second Grade Skills

Syllables. This is a good place to start working with
syllables. Initially, *suh-tuh-er-eet* for *street*, has four syllables. After the blend idea is understood and the second
part of the word has been revealed, the child can hear
that there is only one sound present, *street*.

Second graders start to come across longer words in
their reading, so it is helpful to teach them how to break
up a word into components, or *syllables*.

Syllables are extremely helpful in sounding out
words. A long word can be too daunting for a beginning
reader, causing him to give up, whereas knowing the
syllables lets him see the *smaller parts* that make up
the whole.

You can see how words grow and become more complex by adding more syllables:

> fact; per•fect; per•fec•tion; per•fec•tion•ist;
> per•fec•tion•ism.

Compound Words. Compound words are important because they are a cultural shorthand in English.
They encapsulate whole ideas into two words. Exercises

where the child takes two pictures and uses them to form a single word are helpful in getting him to see the breakdown of a word, as well as its origin. With a strong foundation in both suffixes and compound words, a child will make fewer reading and spelling mistakes such as *neckless* for *necklace*.

Prefixes. Children learn word endings in the 1st grade for grammatical changes—plurals (*-s*), past tense (*-ed*), continuous (*-ing*), etc. In the 2nd grade, they learn how to put two words together to form a third word with compound nouns. Then, once the idea of breaking up a word is clear, the advancing reader can learn a category for vocabulary, such as the prefix *pre-*, rather than learning case by case.

un-	un•happy, un•usual, un•known
dis-	dis•like, dis•honest, dis•appear
ad-	ad•monish, ad•vocate
re-	re•port, re•read, re•play

Suffixes. Earlier, children learned the grammatical endings. There is another category of endings called suffixes, which are the opposite of prefixes. Whereas the suffixes are common, the actual meanings are abstract, so the child can forego learning the meaning at this point.

-ment	excite•ment, apart•ment
-ish	baby•ish, green•ish, self•ish
-tion	condi•tion, situa•tion, inven•tion
-tain	cap•tain, moun•tain, foun•tain

Contractions. When a 2nd grader speaks, contractions come quite naturally, but they can give pause to even an advancing reader. Children often wonder what letter is left out and where the apostrophe goes. The main rule is quite simple: The two words are joined and the apostrophe replaces the letter(s) that has been removed.

With *negatives*, leave out the O in *not = n't*.

is not	isn't	are not	aren't
was not	wasn't	were not	weren't
do not	don't	does not	doesn't
did not	didn't	will not	won't
has not	hasn't	have not	haven't

Positives:

you are	you're	they are	they're
we are	we're	I am	I'm
he is	he's	it is	it's
I have	I've	I had	I'd
I will	I'll	I would	I'd

Homonyms. An area of confusion for many young readers is *homonyms*, where two words that sound the same and are spelled the same have two completely different and unrelated meanings. However, 2nd graders should be becoming proficient at understanding confusing homonyms by the context. Here are some common homonyms:

bear	to carry; the animal (grizzly bear)
suit	to be agreeable to; clothing
bat	a flying animal, a baseball bat

Third Grade

Basic Skills

A 3rd grader can be expected to read a designated 3rd grade text fluently and with expression—using the voice to indicate the *meaning* of the text (emotion and contrast), as well as the *grammatical* indications (question or statement, beginnings or endings, listing, commas and exclamation marks).

Expression and Meaning. Reading with *expression* is relating feeling, emphasis and meaning, based on both vocabulary and pronunciation. It is typical of a 2nd grader to read on regardless of punctuation, and this is perfectly acceptable at that level.

A 3rd grader should read with expression that fully reflects the punctuation.

Help your child read the following sentences:

1 **Statement**   It's here.

2 **Question**   It's here?

3 **Exclamation**   It's here!

4 **Beginning/End** As I said, it's still here.

5 **Listing**   It's here, there, and everywhere.

6 **Quotes**   "It's here!" said Bob.

Phrasing and Comprehension

Word-by-word reading is so choppy that it is hard to understand the meaning of it. If you teach your child to read in phrases, not only will it make his reading clearer to the listener, but his own comprehension will improve. The first step to reading in phrases is to use the punctuation. Pause at a comma, and stop at a period.

He came, he saw, he conquered.

For a child first learning to read, there is the technique of finding the small words within a longer word—*fan•tas•tic*. You can use a similar technique to find the small phrases in a longer sentence. Start each phrase within a sentence with a preposition (in, at, for, by, to, with, etc.).

I drove <u>to the store</u> <u>in a red car</u> <u>on Friday morning</u>.

Understanding the Context

Reflecting the expanding vocabulary of the typical eight-year-old, the reader should be able to go through a text and figure out any new words through the context. For example, if he sees the sentence, *"After the rain, the hill was so muddy and **wuggy** that the hikers all slid to the bottom,"* he should figure out that the nonsense word *wuggy* could mean *slippery* or *wet* or *crumbly*. The clues would be *rain, muddy* and *slid*.

Main Idea

A third-grader should be able to read a whole chapter book (rather than just a paragraph or short story) and talk about the main ideas in it. At this level, there are longer, more difficult words and longer, more difficult sentences. There are more details and more complex ideas to absorb.

If, at any point, you discover that your child is having trouble grasping the main idea of what he reads, use examples such as figuring out the moral of each of the Aesop's Fables or other familiar stories.

"Why did the fox say that the grapes were sour?"

"What happened when the boy cried 'wolf' too many times? Has anything like this ever happened to you?"

"What would a wolf in sheep's clothing be in real life?"

"What was the point of the dog in the manger? What did the dog want? What did the cow want? Who was fair or unfair?"

Another way to clearly determine the main idea of a text is to change the statement to a question. If the answer is *yes*, you have found the main idea. For example, suppose you are trying to choose between the following two main idea choices.

Dogs are greedy.

It's wrong not to share something that you can't use yourself.

Convert each one to a question and see which works.

Are dogs greedy? No, not particularly.

Is it wrong not to share something that you can't use yourself? Yes.

If both sentences are true, choose the larger, more important truth.

It's wrong not to share something that you can't use yourself. *(True, and to the point.)*

Drawing Conclusions

Conclusions become more developed and are based on subtler cues in the language. Texts from which conclusions can be drawn include chapter books, simple newspaper articles, instruction sheets, and children's magazines. A typical conclusion statement by a child is, "You can tell that..." For example, upon reading the following: *The petting zoo was broken into and three animals were missing. Later that week, the animal control officers found a chicken, a duck, and a rabbit from the petting zoo.* The conclusion can be drawn that all three animals were found. A child could say, *"You can tell that they found all three of them because they listed three animals at the end."*

Making Inferences

Bobby was furious. He was holding his crumpled test paper in his hand. "I studied hard," he yelled. "Look at this test!" Knowing what the reader knows about studying and taking tests, plus what the story tells, what must have happened? It would be an informed guess to say that Bobby had not done well on the test. Perhaps earlier in the book, however, the reader had learned that Bobby was a perfectionist, so he could be that upset about missing only one question.

Sequencing

This is a very important skill in terms of using sequential or chronological logic to create order in events. A child with clarity of thought will have an easier time with both reading and writing, not to mention math and history. Third graders can be expected to understand flashbacks, stories told in different orders by different characters and the thread of a story related through a series of letters or newspaper articles. It helps a child to practice articulating this skill with everyday situations, such as a movie or typical school day (including subjects, recess, sports, and what the teacher did, and when.) They say, "Start at the beginning," but the beginning is frequently the hardest part to determine. Practice with, "What happens first?"

Projecting an Outcome

After hearing or reading of a series of events, a third-grader should be able to predict what migh happen next. This is not only a type of inference, but a good indicator of how well a child understands sequencing, the main idea, and the facts of the story up to that point.

Getting the Facts

This is an extension of a 2nd grade skill. It should include the five W's in more depth, with more adjectives and descriptive vocabulary, as well as numbers, dates, personal and place names, and both figurative and literal information (*He felt the logs* vs. *His legs felt like logs*).

Self-correction

It's vital to reread and cross-check for facts and ideas. At this age, children are reluctant to go back over something they have completed once, but by doing so they will pick up important facts that they missed, as well as garner a clearer understanding of the main idea. This is also the point where children need to look up any unknown words that they can't figure out from the context. One 3rd grader, who enjoyed stories about England tried to figure out *knickers* from the context. Since people were always putting them on before they went out, he figured they were boots—until he came across a reference to a plaid pair! Then he figured he'd better look the word up in a dictionary.

Writing

In addition to getting the facts and ideas from reading, it is at the 3rd grade level that writing starts to gain sophistication. Of course, children will have been putting various forms of ideas on paper since kindergarten, but from this level on, the output is expected to increase and improve. They need to come up with their own facts, main ideas, conclusions and inferences.

The more a child reads, the more familiar he will be with the conventions of printed materials, including paragraphs, punctuation, capitalization, indenting and spelling.

Fourth Grade

Basic Skills

A 4th grader should be able to identify a piece as nonfiction, fiction, drama, or poetry. The prefixes *ex-*, *mis-*, *dis-*, *uni-*, *bi-*, and *tri-*, and the suffixes *-ous*, *-ship*, and *-ness*, should be recognized easily. They should know the difference between a fact and a simile (a simile is a phrase using like or as, such as he is as hungry as a horse or she ran like the wind). Young readers should be able to read visual presentations, such as diagrams, charts, and maps to categorize and understand information. They should know where a topic sentence generally occurs and how key words relate to the topic. Hand in hand with their writing skills, they should recognize the three main types of writing—informative, descriptive, and persuasive. They need to recognize and understand recurring themes in fiction, such as friendship, honor, death, dealing with adversity, etc.

There is a big dividing line between 3rd and 4th grades—through 3rd grade a child is learning to read, whereas from the 4th grade on, a child is reading to learn. This means that children have learned the basics, and are ready to take on the reading tasks of analysis, synthesis, summary, restating, contrast and comparison. They need to use context to find information that isn't expressly stated in the text, such as time and place.

Main Idea and Getting the Facts

A 4th grader should be able to read a text and summarize the most important points, without getting tangled in the details. He also needs to recognize and extract the facts.

Drawing Conclusions

In a story, the writer doesn't spell out every last detail. There are things that a reader will need to figure out or guess at. Earlier, we saw only **conclusions**, which are drawn from information given.

He did it again!

The word *again* allows you to conclude that something has happened before. Conclusions are logical deductions, based on evidence. It is necessary that the author has provided all the required information. A common syllogism is:

All men are mortal.
Socrates is a man.
Therefore, Socrates is mortal.

Making Inferences

Inferences, on the other hand, are *educated guesses* that the reader makes based on what the writer says *plus* what the reader knows.

A child comes home from school. He goes up the walk and into the house. "Hey! Dad! I'm hungry!"

The writer doesn't say that he went into his own house, but the reader can figure out that he did. Nor does he say that the father was home, but you can guess that he was.

Analysis and Evaluation

This is a more advanced skill. Children are called upon to make higher level distinctions. Earlier, child distinguished between fantasy and reality. At this stage, they determine the degree to which the plot is realistic. This is a good place for a child to bring in this own experience. An older person might read a story about teenagers and find it perfectly plausible, whereas a young person, with his own perspective and relativity to the age group, might be able to point out aspects that don't ring true.

Furthermore, readers can begin to analyze the author's word choice and topic. Does the author use positive words for a group of people or disparage a group of people? What references to age, gender, occupation, race, intelligence, or feelings are made and what is implied by them. Some authors bring up images of nature, whereas others have more urban settings. Newspapers are a good place to examine bias through the presentation of information. What is brought up first? What is buried at the end of the article? How do the photographs shape the words that accompany them? And so on.

Word Roots

Students can start expanding their vocabularies, improving their comprehension, and understanding spelling changes by knowing a few basic Latin root words and their prefixes.

With this knowledge, readers can make educated guesses at the meaning of a word based on its origins. This will supplement the information derived from the context. They will also have a better understanding of some of the spelling shifts that take place. For example, B/P and C/G/Q shift back and forth (*describe* to *descriptive second* to *sequence* to *segue distinct* to *distinguish*). Prefixes shift toward alliteration (*un•legal* is *illegal*, *ad•similate* is *assimilate*, *con•port* is *comport*, *sub•ceptible* is *susceptible*). I and Y trade off frequently (*pony* to *ponies*, *easy* to *easily*).

Fifth Grade

Basic Skills

A 5th grade reader should be familiar with common genres of literature such as mysteries, biographies, folk tales, fantasy, science fiction and nonfiction, and recognize how each one shapes the stories of information presented in them.

In terms of *comprehension*, 5th-graders are in a position to state the main idea of a passage from a 5th-grade reading book, extracting the pertinent details and weeding out the irrelevant ones. Additionally, they should be able to talk *about* the story, as well as retell it in their own words.

They should figure out the meaning of new and difficult words by the *context*, and correct their own mistakes by using the context.

They should be able to identify *cause* and *effect* in either fiction or nonfiction works.

By looking even beyond the main idea, they should be able to tell what the *author's purpose* was—why he wrote that particular book, told that particular story and used those particular words to do it.

Based on their own lives, they should also be capable of seeing relationships between their own experiences and those depicted in the work, thus deriving a deeper understanding of what the author was trying to say.

They should easily identify the setting by location and relationship to the characters. They can think about how the story would have changed if it had been moved from one place in the world to another.

They should be able to tell if the plot is realistic or not, and whether a character could be a real person or not, based on the reasons for a character's actions, taking into account the situation and motivation of the person portrayed. It should be clear whether it is a stereotypical representation of a person or a fully developed and characterized individual. The characters should be identified by name, occupation, appearance, age, temperament, etc. With this understanding of the character, readers should be able to take on a character's perspective and explain his point of view.

Students need to recognize how the structure supports a story. If it is an epistolary novel, how do the letters contribute to the understanding of the book? If it is told in flashbacks, how does this build up to a complete understanding of the plot? Are there metaphors or similes?

Readers should be developing favorite authors, as well as opinions on the works they have read. With these authors, they should be able to identify themes within each book, as well as from book to book. They should be able to compare and contrast books by the same author, along with books from different authors.

Finally, they should be familiar with the major genres, and recognize how this shapes the materials presented in them.

Reference Skills

Reference skills should include outlining and note taking; recognizing fiction and nonfiction; using reference texts such as the dictionary, thesaurus, encyclopedia, world almanac, and telephone book; and using the card catalogue, as well as various book sections of the library. They should recognize and use the reference sections within a book such as the table of contents, index, glossary, and bibliography.

Reading Reassessments

Kindergarten through Fifth Grade

Matching Pictures

Kindergarten

Look at the picture on the left. Draw a circle around the matching picture in the box.

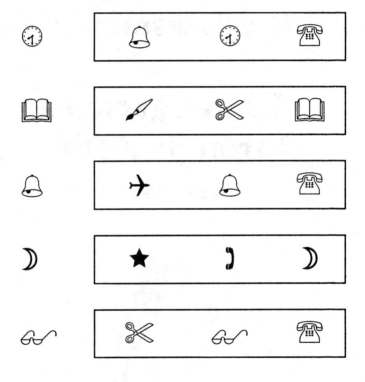

0-1 ✗, enter date in chart on page 85 and go to the next page; 2 or more ✗'s, stop test and go to Guidelines on page 87. Retest at a later date.

Matching Letters

Look at the letter on the left. Draw a circle around the matching letter in the box.

D | B   D   W

K | A   N   K

J | J   I   L

X | R   Y   X

F | E   F   Y

0-1 ✘, enter date in chart on page 85 and go to the next page; 2 or more ✘'s, stop test and go to Guidelines on page 87. Retest at a later date.

Context

Circle the picture that best finishes each sentence.

We took a trip in the

I was reading a good

The teacher ate her

 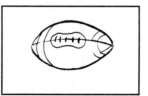

0-1 ✗, enter date in chart on page 85 and go to the next page; 2 or more ✗'s, stop test and go to Guidelines on page 87. Retest at a later date.

Fact Finding

Look at the picture and tell if each sentence is TRUE or FALSE.

	True	**False**
1. The dog is playing with his friends.	❑	❑
2. The dog is bouncing a ball.	❑	❑
3. The dog is taller than the bush.	❑	❑

0-1 ✗, enter date in chart on page 85 and go on to the next page; 2 or more ✗'s, stop test and go to Guidelines on page 87. Retest at a later date.

Story Order

Kindergarten

Look at the four pictures. Decide what order they should be in to tell a story. Write numbers in the little boxes to show the order the pictures belong in.

Correct order, enter date in chart on page 85 and go to the next page; incorrect order, stop test and go to Guidelines on page 87. Retest at a later date.

Story Sense

Kindergarten

Look at the top pictures. Draw a circle around the bottom picture that shows what is more likely to happen next.

Correct response, enter date in chart on page 85 and go to the next page; incorrect response, stop test and go to Guidelines on page 87. Retest at a later date.

Context

Choose the word that best finishes the sentence.

1. We put jam on the _____.

   ❑ bread   ❑ air   ❑ lots

2. Selma took a _____.

   ❑ next   ❑ funny   ❑ bath

3. The story was very _____.

   ❑ good   ❑ does   ❑ tall

0-1 ✖, enter date in chart on page 85 and go to the next page; 2 or more ✖'s, stop test and go to Guidelines on page 87. Retest at a later date.

Fact Finding   *First Grade*

Read the paragraph and tell if each sentence below is
TRUE or FALSE.

> I am a toy. I am big and
> round. I can bounce. I am made
> of rubber. I am a ball.

		True	**False**
1.	The toy is square.	❏	❏
2.	The toy is big.	❏	❏
3.	The toy is a car.	❏	❏

0-1 ✗, enter date in chart on page 85 and go to the next
page; 2 or more ✗'s, stop test and go to Guidelines on
page 87. Retest at a later date.

Main Idea

Read the following paragraph to your child and have her answer the question that follows.

> Susan looked in the cookie jar. It was empty. She had really wanted a chocolate chip cookie. Susan was disappointed. She had a bowl of corn flakes instead.

What is the main idea?

- ❑ Susan was disappointed.
- ❑ Susan wanted a cookie.
- ❑ Susan had corn flakes.

Reading	❑ fluent	❑ halting
Speed	❑ less than 1 minute	❑ more than 1 minute
Vocabulary	❑ 0-3 unknown wds.	❑ 3+ unknown words
Response	❑ correct	❑ incorrect

Correct response, enter date in chart on page 85 and go to the next page; incorrect response, stop test and go to Guidelines on page 87. Retest at a later date.

Conclusions

Read the following paragraph to your child and have her answer the question that follows.

> Sally has always wanted to visit a farm. Today she finally got a chance to visit one. While she was there, she got to ride a horse and see cows, pigs, and ducks. Sally said, "I wish I could live on a farm."

Which sentence describes Sally?

❑ Sally has dark curly hair.

❑ Sally has a pet duck.

❑ Sally likes the farm.

Reading	❑ fluent	❑ halting
Speed	❑ less than 1 minute	❑ more than 1 minute
Vocabulary	❑ 0-3 unknown words	❑ 3+ unknown words
Response	❑ correct	❑ incorrect

Correct response, enter date in chart on page 85 and go to the next page; incorrect response, stop test and go to Guidelines on page 87. Retest at a later date.

Context   *Second Grade*

Choose the word that best completes each sentence.

1. The cheetah can run much faster than a person. It is known for its _____.

   ❑ speed   ❑ teeth   ❑ height

2. In Japan, they do not always cook their fish. They like to eat it _____.

   ❑ today   ❑ outdoors   ❑ raw

3. When you are sleepy, it is hard to keep your _____ open.

   ❑ eyes   ❑ door   ❑ window

4. When will the snow _____?

   ❑ white   ❑ fall   ❑ spill

5. I want to go to the beach and _____.

   ❑ tree   ❑ swim   ❑ visit

> 0-1 ✕, enter date in chart on page 85 and go to the next page; 2 or more ✕'s, stop test and go to Guidelines on page 87. Retest at a later date.

Fact Finding

Read the following paragraph and tell if each sentence is TRUE or FALSE.

Spiders have eight legs. Did you know that they also have eight eyes? Many people are afraid of spiders, but spiders are helpful to us. Without spiders there would be too many bugs. Spiders are also known as arachnids.

	True	False
1. Spiders have more legs than eyes.	☐	☐
2. Spiders can be helpful to people.	☐	☐
3. Without spiders, there would be lots of bugs.	☐	☐
4. Spiders are also known as amphibians.	☐	☐

0-1 ✖, enter date in chart on page 85 and go to the next page; 2 or more ✖'s, stop test and go to Guidelines on page 87. Retest at a later date.

Main Idea   *Second Grade*

Read the following story and tell what the main idea is.

Sports

Many kids like to play team sports. When you play on a team, you have to work with other people. Some people try to score points alone. They think it will be their point. Points made in team sports are team points. If you don't want to share the points you make then you should play golf.

The main idea is:

❏ Any point made is for the whole team.

❏ Some players score their own points.

❏ Golf is fun.

Reading	❏ fluent	❏ halting
Speed	❏ less than 1 minute	❏ more than 1 minute
Vocabulary	❏ 0-3 unknown wds.	❏ 3+ unknown wds.
Response	❏ correct	❏ incorrect

Correct response, enter date in chart on page 85 and go to the next page; incorrect response, stop test and go to Guidelines on page 87. Retest at a later date.

Conclusions

Second Grade

Read the following story and answer the questions that follow.

Dolphins

Dolphins do not sleep like we do. They take many short naps. Like us, dolphins breathe air. But dolphins live in the sea. Dolphins can talk under water.

How are dolphins and people the same?

❑ They sleep like we do.

❑ They breathe air.

❑ They live in the sea.

Reading	❑ fluent	❑ halting
Speed	❑ less than 1 minute	❑ more than 1 minute
Vocabulary	❑ 0-3 unknown wds.	❑ 3+ unknown wds.
Responses	❑ correct	❑ incorrect

Correct response, enter date in chart on page 85 and go to the next page; incorrect response, stop test and go to Guidelines on page 87. Retest at a later date.

Context
Third Grade

Choose the words that best complete the sentences.

1. Have you ever wondered how a fly can walk on the
_____ (a) ? It is because it has _____ (b)
hairs on its feet that keep it from falling.

    (a) ❏ heat   ❏ ceiling   ❏ third
    (b) ❏ wall   ❏ one   ❏ sticky

2. When you look at an iceberg, you can only see the
tip. An iceberg is nine _____ (a) bigger than the
part you can see. Most of it is under _____ (b) .

    (a) ❏ times   ❏ lives   ❏ more
    (b) ❏ air   ❏ water   ❏ land

3. In America, it is very common to shake hands
when you meet _____ (a). In Japan, it is more
usual to bow to a person. There may be differences,
but good _____ (b) are very important in both
countries.

    (a) ❏ something   ❏ new   ❏ someone
    (b) ❏ food   ❏ manners   ❏ handshake

4. Anteaters don't only eat ants. They also eat termites and other _____ (a). Anteaters have no teeth but have a long, sticky _____ (b) that can be up to two feet long!

(a) ❑ rugs   ❑ insects   ❑ anteaters
(b) ❑ tongue   ❑ anthill   ❑ eye

5. Bears hibernate all winter. They sleep in a _____ (a) and don't eat for several months. They live off of their body fat. It stands to _____ (b) that when they finally wake up they are hungry and grouchy!

(a) ❑ rock   ❑ cave   ❑ winter
(b) ❑ eat   ❑ wake   ❑ reason

0-2 ✘'s, enter date in chart on page 85 and go to the next page; 3 or more ✘'s, stop test and go to Guidelines on page 87. Retest at a later date.

Fact Finding
Third Grade

Read the following paragraph and tell if each sentence is TRUE or FALSE.

Nowadays, people use many machines every day. One of the earliest machines was a very simple one. Let's see if you can guess what it was. It was not invented until the Bronze Age in Europe.

At first, it was made of round, wooden disks. In 2700 BC, spokes were added. That was almost 5,000 years ago. Do you know what this simple machine is? It is the wheel!

		True	False
1.	The earliest wheel was made with spokes.	❑	❑
2.	The wheel was invented 2,700 years ago.	❑	❑
3.	The wheel is not a machine.	❑	❑
4.	The first wheel was made of bronze.	❑	❑
5.	The wheel was invented in Europe.	❑	❑

0-1 ✖, enter date in chart on page 85 and go to the next page; 2 or more ✖'s, stop test and go to Guidelines on page 87. Retest at a later date.

Main Idea   *Third Grade*

Read the following paragraphs and tell what the main idea is.

Trees

Trees are not just the huge plants you see growing in a forest. A large part of the tree grows under the ground. This part is called the roots. If the tree is big and really old, the roots may reach down 100 feet!

The roots hold the tree into the ground. Without roots, trees would fall over! The roots do another important job for the tree. They gather minerals and water from the soil to feed the tree so it will grow. Most land plants could not live without roots to support them and to feed them.

The main idea is:

❑ The roots of the tree are underground.

❑ The roots do important jobs for the tree.

❑ Roots can grow to be 100 feet long.

Reading	❑ fluent	❑ halting
Speed	❑ less than 1 minute	❑ more than 1 minute
Vocabulary	❑ 0-3 unknown wds.	❑ 3+ unknown wds.
Response	❑ correct	❑ incorrect

Correct response, enter date in chart on page 85 and go to the next page; incorrect response, stop test and go to Guidelines on page 87. Retest at a later date.

Conclusions   *Third Grade*

Read the following paragraphs and answer the question that follows.

Pet Grasshoppers

Believe it or not, some people keep grasshoppers as pets. It's important to always keep two of them together. Otherwise, the grasshoppers would get lonely!

People keep grasshoppers in a jar filled with dirt. The dirt helps grasshoppers feel like they are at home. They need a screen over the jar to let air in. The screen also keeps the grasshoppers in! Instead of a screen, some people use a small net or a cheesecloth. They make sure there is room under the screen for the grasshoppers to hop! Grasshoppers are clean, quiet pets.

When you have a pet grasshopper, it is important to

❑ Keep it quiet.
❑ Provide it with all the things it needs.
❑ Use a cheesecloth.

Reading	❑ fluent	❑ halting
Speed	❑ less than 1 minute	❑ more than 1 minute
Vocabulary	❑ 0-3 unknown wds.	❑ 3+ unknown wds.
Response	❑ correct	❑ incorrect

Correct response, enter date in chart on page 85 and go to the next page; incorrect response, stop test and go to Guidelines on page 87. Retest at a later date.

Context

Choose the words that best complete the sentences.

1. The giraffe is the tallest animal. A _____ (a) giraffe can be up to 18 feet tall. They browse in treetops at heights that other animals can't reach. They can _____ (b) most of their enemies and have been known to kill lions with a single powerful kick.

   (a) ❑ few   ❑ another   ❑ male
   (b) ❑ follow   ❑ outrun   ❑ play

2. Table tennis is a game, usually played indoors, by two or four _____ (a) . It is like a miniature game of tennis. It is also called Ping-Pong. The regulation game is played on a table that measures 9 feet by 5 feet, and is 2.5 feet high. A 6-inch net _____ (b) the table in two.

   (a) ❑ referees   ❑ players   ❑ games
   (b) ❑ includes   ❑ falls   ❑ divides

3. The carnivorous fish called the piranha is _____ (a) to the catfish. Piranha are found in Africa and the Amazon. They have powerful jaws and _____ (b) sharp triangular teeth, capable of killing humans and cattle.

   (a) ❑ known   ❑ related   ❑ fiercer
   (b) ❑ razor   ❑ round   ❑ heavy

4. In the ancient Roman religion, Neptune was the god of water. In later times, he was _____ (a) with the Greek god of the sea, Poseidon. The 8th _____ (b) from the sun is named after him.

    (a) ❑ identified   ❑ exclaimed   ❑ divided
    (b) ❑ star   ❑ planet   ❑ moon

5. World War I began in 1914 and was touched off by the _____ (a) of Archduke Ferdinand of Austria. The Allies (Great Britain, France, Russia, Serbia, Belgium, Italy, Portugal, Romania and America) _____ (b) the Central Powers (Germany, Austria-Hungary and Bulgaria). The Allies finally won in 1918.

    (a) ❑ invention   ❑ President   ❑ assassination
    (b) ❑ discussed   ❑ fought   ❑ introduced

0-2 ✘'s, enter date in chart on page 85 and go to the next page; 3 or more ✘'s, stop test and go to Guidelines on page 87. Retest at a later date.

Fact Finding

Read the following paragraph and tell if each sentence is TRUE or FALSE.

Confucius was an ancient Chinese philosopher. He was born around 500 BC in Lu, a former feudal state in China.

He was upset by the constant fighting between the Chinese states and the corruption and greed of the rulers, so he supported a moral system that would preserve peace and give the people a stable, fair government.

After this death, his philosophy became a religion called Confucianism, which had ideas similar to the Golden Rule. He believed that people should be treated they way they themselves would like to be treated.

	True	**False**
1. Confucius changed his name to Lu.	❏	❏
2. Before Confucius was a philosopher, he was a warrior.	❏	❏
3. Confucius' philosophy is quite different from the Golden Rule.	❏	❏
4. Confucius thought that rulers were corrupt.	❏	❏
5. During his lifetime, Confucius turned his philosophy into a religion.	❏	❏

0-1 ✖, enter date in chart on page 85 and go to the next page; 2 or more ✖'s, stop test and go to Guidelines on page 87. Retest at a later date.

Main Idea   *Fourth Grade*

Read the following story and tell what the main idea is.

One day, a rabbit met a lion in the woods. The lion was hungry and irritable. He said, "Don't move! I'm going to eat you up." While he was talking, the lion backed the rabbit up against a rock. The rabbit realized she couldn't run away. "I'll have to use my brain instead of my legs," she thought.

Aloud to the lion, the rabbit said calmly, "I would have made a good lunch for you last month. But I've had eight babies since then. I have to look for food all day long in order to feed them." "Stop!" the lion interrupted. "I don't care how many children you have. I'm going to eat you right now." The lion stepped closer to the rabbit.

"Wait!" yelled the rabbit. "Look how thin I am. I ran off all my fat looking for food for my children. But I know where you can find something delicious!" The lion sat back to hear what the rabbit had to say. "There's an old well not far from here. There's a big piece of cheese in the bottom of it. Come on, I'll show you."

The lion followed closely after the rabbit, making sure she couldn't run away. "See," said the rabbit when they got to the well. Inside the well was what looked like a round, yellow piece of cheese. It was really the reflection of the moon, but the lion didn't know this. The lion leaned over the well, wondering how to get the cheese. The rabbit jumped up and quickly pushed the lion in. "I am a clever little thing," the rabbit thought as she hopped home to her children.

The main idea is:

❑ The rabbit was trapped, but used her brains to trick the lion and escape.

❑ The lion was irritable and wanted to eat.

❑ The moon's reflection looks like a piece of cheese.

Reading	❑ fluent	❑ halting
Speed	❑ less than 1 minute	❑ more than 1 minute
Vocabulary	❑ 0-3 unknown wds.	❑ 3+ unknown wds.
Response	❑ correct	❑ incorrect

Correct response, enter date in chart on page 85 and go to the next page; incorrect response, stop test and go to Guidelines on page 87. Retest at a later date.

Conclusions
Fourth Grade

Read the following story and tell what the conclusion is.

One day, the hare and the tortoise were talking. Actually, the hare was bragging and the tortoise was listening. "I run faster than the wind," boasted the hare. "I pity you because you are the slowest thing I've ever seen!"

"Oh, really?" asked the tortoise with a smile. "Let's race to the other side of the meadow."

"Ha!" laughed the hare. "You must be joking! You'll lose! Well, if you insist, let's race."

"I'm on my way," the tortoise said, and started walking slowly and steadily across the meadow. The hare stood there and laughed. "How sad! That slowpoke wants to compete with me!" he said. "I'll take a little nap while that poor old tortoise plods along. When I wake up, he'll still only be halfway there." Some time later, the hare woke up. He saw that while he had been sleeping, the tortoise had won the race.

The best way to get reach a goal is

❑ By working hard and not giving up.

❑ By sleeping first to get some rest.

❑ By thinking you're better than others.

Reading	❑ fluent	❑ halting
Speed	❑ less than 1 minute	❑ more than 1 minute
Vocabulary	❑ 0-3 unknown wds.	❑ 3+ unknown wds.
Response	❑ correct	❑ incorrect

Correct response, enter date in chart on page 85 and go to the next page; incorrect response, stop test and go to Guidelines on page 87. Retest at a later date.

....

Context

Choose the words that best complete the sentences.

1. Tidal waves are seismic sea waves or tsunami. They are catastrophic ocean waves generated by submarine movements such as earthquakes, volcanic _____ (a) or landslides beneath the ocean. Tsunamis can travel at speeds up to 450 miles per hour. When they approach _____ (b) water, their height can rise to as high as 100 feet.

(a) ❑ volcanoes   ❑ speeds   ❑ eruptions
(b) ❑ dry   ❑ shallow   ❑ tsunami

2. Hummingbirds feed on insects and the nectar of flowers, for which their long, _____ (a) bills are especially adapted. They are usually seen hovering or darting as they feed in flight. Their wingbeats are so rapid (50-75 beats per second) that their wings appear _____ (b) .

(a) ❑ slender   ❑ invisible   ❑ expensive
(b) ❑ falling   ❑ old   ❑ blurred

3. Alfred Nobel invented dynamite. He was, however, a pacifist who regretted the _____ (a) power that he had created. He _____ (b) the Nobel Prize as an award for outstanding achievement in physics, chemistry, medicine, peace, literature, and economics.

(a) ❑ kind   ❑ sweet   ❑ destructive
(b) ❑ established   ❑ said   ❑ blamed

4. In 1943, Jacques Cousteau invented the _____ (a), also known as a self-contained underwater breathing apparatus (scuba). He also founded the French navy's undersea research group. He made many _____ (b) films about his work before his death in 1997.

(a) ❏ aqualung ❏ fertilizer ❏ shark cage
(b) ❏ automobile ❏ documentary ❏ music

5. The New York City Ballet is one of the _____ (a) American dance companies of the 20th century. It was founded by Lincoln Kirstein and George Balanchine in 1946. The company developed a distinctly American style of dancing by combining Italian, French, and Russian _____ (b) with a unique musical flair.

(a) ❏ foremost ❏ American ❏ ballet
(b) ❏ engineers ❏ columns ❏ traditions

0-2 ✘'s, enter date in chart on page 85 and go to the next page; 3 or more ✘'s, stop test and go to Guidelines on page 87. Retest at a later date.

Fact Finding

Read the following paragraph and tell if each sentence is TRUE or FALSE.

Dr. Martin Luther King was a preacher and civil rights leader. He was born in 1929 and died in 1968. He led a boycott against the city bus lines because of their segregation policy.

Because of his philosophy of nonviolent resistance, he was arrested several times in the 1950s and 1960s. In 1963, he organized the March on Washington, which brought more than 200,000 people together. In 1964, he was awarded the Nobel Peace Prize.

In 1968, he was shot and killed by an assassin's bullet on the balcony of the motel where he was staying. James Earl Ray was convicted of his murder.

		True	**False**
1.	Martin Luther King led a bus boycott because of the poor service.	❑	❑
2.	Dr. King was a civil rights leader, preacher, and Nobel prize winner.	❑	❑
3.	Dr. King assassinated James Earl Ray.	❑	❑
4.	Dr. King believed that violence was not an effective way to accomplish goals.	❑	❑
5.	Dr. King could not get anyone to march on Washington.	❑	❑

0-1 ✖, enter date in chart on page 85 and go to the next page; 2 or more ✖'s, stop test and go to Guidelines on page 87. Retest at a later date.

Main Idea

Read the following story and tell what the main idea is.

As long as there have been people, they have wanted to move from one place to the next. Until the wheel was invented, they had to walk or ride horses. In some parts of the world, wealthy people had other people carry them around in palanquins. With the invention of the wheel, however, the possibilities for transportation multiplied. When railroads became the major means of transportation, they replaced earlier types of travel such as the stagecoach and horse drawn wagon. Railroads were the main form of transportation in America for a hundred years, but starting in the early 1900s, they have had to deal with competition from other forms of transportation.

These days, millions of people own cars. Buses are an inexpensive mode of travel and readily accessible. Eighteen-wheel trucks are used for transporting merchandise. Airplanes offer fast transportation over long distances. Due to these alternatives, there has been a steep decline in the use of trains.

Almost all railroads have serious problems that could push them out of business. On the other hand, railroads provide low-cost, fuel-saving transportation that will always be important.

The main idea is:

❏ When railroads became the main form of transportation, they took the place of other means of travel.

❏ Starting in the early 1900s, railroads have dealt with competition from other forms of transportation.

❏ Even though there are many modes of transportation available today, trains continue to be very useful and valuable.

Reading	❏ fluent	❏ halting
Speed	❏ less than 1 minute	❏ more than 1 minute
Vocabulary	❏ 0-3 unknown wds.	❏ 3+ unknown wds.
Response	❏ correct	❏ incorrect

Correct response, enter date in chart on page 85 and go to the next page; incorrect response, stop test and go to Guidelines on page 87. Retest at a later date.

Conclusions

Fifth Grade

Read the following story and answer the question.

For many years in the late 1800s, strong men gave their lives to the railroad tracks that criss-cross the United States. They worked and sweat to lay thousands of miles of track that carried passengers and freight from one coast to the other. The strongest of these men was the hammerman John Henry. He could drive steel and lay track faster, better, and straighter than any other man alive.

Around 1870, the steam drill was invented. One day, another company on the far side of a mountain decided to dig a tunnel using the steam drill. John Henry was matched against the best man from that company to see who would reach the middle of the mountain first. To make a long story short, John Henry beat the steam drill by four feet! That night, he said, "I was a steel driving man." Then he lay down and closed his eyes forever.

How did John Henry feel the night he won the contest?

- ❑ Excited that he'd won a valuable prize.
- ❑ Like he had accomplished his goal.
- ❑ Ready for another contest soon.

Reading	❑ fluent	❑ halting
Speed	❑ less than 1 minute	❑ more than 1 minute
Vocabulary	❑ 0-3 unknown wds.	❑ 3+ unknown wds.
Response	❑ correct	❑ incorrect

Correct response, enter date in chart on page 85 and go to the next page; incorrect response, stop test and go to Guidelines on page 87. Retest at a later date.

Answer Key

Assessments

68-69   **1.** (a) eat, (b) fast   **4.** (a) luck, (b) mirror
        2. (a) food, (b) tails   **5.** (a) safety, (b) down
        3. (a) poisonous, (b) sick

73-74   **1.** (a) breathes, (b) water   **4.** (a) Marsupial, (b) called
        2. (a) Ocean, (b) volcanoes **5.** (a) animals, (b) invertebrate
        3. (a) black, (b) diamonds

78-79   **1.** (a) warriors, (b) period   **4.** (a) artery, (b) microscopic
        2. (a) composing, (b) category **5.** (a) pierced (b) drawing
        3. (a) ruled, (b) dynasty

81-82 Antarctica has been a source of fascination...
83-84 1. living on land and in the sea
2. fin-footed
3. warm-blooded animal
4. fat
5. cold climates

Reassessments

page
148 1. bread   2. bath   3. good
148 1. false   2. true   3. false
150 Susan was disappointed.
151 Sally likes the farm.
152 1. speed   2. raw   3. eyes   4. fall   5. swim
153 1. false   2. true   3. true   4. false
154 Any point made is for the whole team.
155 They breathe air
156-57 1. (a) ceiling, (b) sticky   4. (a) insects, (b) tongue
2. (a) times, (b) water   5. (a) cave, (b) reason
3. (a) someone, (b) manners
158 1. false   2. false   3. false   4. false   5. true
159 The roots do important jobs for trees.
160 Provide it with all the things it needs.
161-62 1. (a) male, (b) outrun   4. (a) identified, (b) planet
2. (a) players, (b) divides   5. (a) assassination, (b) fought
3. (a) related, (b) razor
163 1. false   2. false   3. false   4. true   5. false
165 The rabbit was trapped, but used her brains to escape.
166 By working hard and not giving up.
167-68 1. (a) eruptions, (b) shallow
2. (a) slender, (b) blurred
3. (a) destructive, (b) established
4. (a) aqualung, (b) documentary
5. (a) foremost, (b) traditions
169 1. false   2. true   3. false   4. true   5. false
171 Even though there are many modes of transportation available today, trains continue to be useful and valuable.
172 Like he had accomplished his goal.

....
174

Appendix 1

NAEP Reading Achievement Standards

The National Assessment of Educational Progress (NAEP), an arm of the U.S. Department of Education, serves the vital function of reporting to educators, parents, policy makers, and the general public how well our students are achieving in the area of reading proficiency.

The 1994 NAEP Reading Assessment was administered to national samples of 4th-, 8th, and 12th-grade students attending public and nonpublic schools, and to samples of fourth graders in the 44 jurisdictions that participated in the 1994 Trial State Assessment. Nearly 140,000 students were assessed in the national and jurisdiction samples. Students' reading performance is described on a proficiency scale ranging from 0 to 500, and in relation to three reading achievement levels: *Basic, Proficient,* and *Advanced.* The assessment results are reported based on the performance of students at each of the three grades and within specific subgroups of the population. For each grade, the definitions are cumulative from *Basic* through *Advanced*. One level builds on the previous level. That is, knowledge at the *Proficient* level presumes mastery of the *Basic* level, and knowledge at the *Advanced* level presumes mastery of both the *Basic* and *Proficient* levels.

Fourth Grade Reading Achievement Levels

Fourth-grade students performing at the *Basic* level should demonstrate an understanding of the overall meaning of what they read. When reading text appropriate for 4th graders, they should be able to make relatively obvious connections between the text and their own experiences, and extend the ideas in the text by making simple inferences.

Fourth-grade students performing at the *Proficient* level should be able to demonstrate an overall understanding of the text, providing inferential as well as literal information. When reading text appropriate to 4th grade, they should be able to extend the ideas in the text by making inferences, drawing conclusions, and making connections to their own experiences. The connection between the text and what the student infers should be clear.

Fourth grade students performing at the *Advanced* level should be able to generalize about topics in the reading selection and demonstrate an awareness of how authors compose and use literary devices. When reading text appropriate to 4th grade, they should be able to judge texts critically and, in general, give thorough answers that indicate careful thought.

Grade 4: NAEP Trial State Assessments in Reading 1994 Assessment, Public Schools Only

State	At or Above Basic	Below Basic
Alabama	52%	48%
Arizona	52%	48%
Arkansas	54%	46%
California	44%	56%
Colorado	59%	41%
Connecticut	68%	32%
Delaware	52%	48%
Florida	50%	50%
Georgia	52%	48%
Hawaii	46%	54%
Indiana	66%	34%
Iowa	69%	31%
Kentucky	56%	44%
Louisiana	40%	60%
Maine	75%	25%
Maryland	55%	45%
Massachusetts	69%	31%
Minnesota	65%	35%
Mississippi	45%	55%
Missouri	62%	38%
Montana	69%	31%
Nebraska	66%	34%
New Hampshire	70%	30%
New Jersey	65%	35%
New Mexico	49%	51%
New York	57%	43%
North Carolina	59%	41%
North Dakota	73%	27%
Pennsylvania	61%	39%
Rhode Island	65%	35%
South Carolina	48%	52%
Tennessee	58%	42%
Texas	58%	42%
Utah	64%	36%
Virginia	57%	43%
Washington	59%	41%
West Virginia	58%	42%
Wisconsin	71%	29%
Wyoming	68%	32%

* NAEP 1994 Reading Report Card for the Nation and the
States. U.S. Dept. of Ed., Office of Educational Research and Improvement

Appendix 2

Online Educational Resources

Activities for Reading & Writing

http://www.ed.gov/Family/RWN/Activ97

This is the basic literacy kit to get children preschool through 6th grade and reading partners started. The kit includes an activities book, a vocabulary log, a bookmark, & two certificates. Every public library in the country will have kits.

National Education Association

http://www.nea.org

Interested in great schools? You've come to the right place. We're the more than 2.3 million members of the National Education Association, and we hope this page can help public education work for every child and every family.

The Learning Partners Guide

http://www.udel.edu/ETL/RWN/Tutorman.html

A guide to tutoring for learning partners to help children develop their reading and writing skills.

The Just Add Kids! Resource Directory
http://www.ed.gov/Family/JustAddKids/
A compilation of national organizations that can be useful in starting & supporting community reading projects. From Just Add Kids.

Family Education Network
http://www.familyeducation.com
This is an interesting site with a lot of information for parents. It is very browsable, like the family magazine that it is.

Early Childhood Educator's and Family Web Corner
http://www.nauticom.net/www/cokids
This sunny site has loads of information—family pages, teacher pages, educational debate, and links to other sites.

The EdWeb K-12 Resource Guide
http://k12.cnidr.org:90/k12.html
This section of EdWeb offers a collection of the best online educational resources available, including lesson plans, interactive projects, and interesting places for kids to explore.

Educational Online Services (EOL)
http://netspace.students.brown.edu/eos/main_image.html
Welcome to the world wide web of educational online sources. We want to make this a space where everyone can contribute and help build a clearinghouse for educational information.

Research and Reference Resources

United States Department of Education
http://www.ed.gov
http://www.ed.gov./index.html
The site of the U.S. Department of Education. It lists news, grant and contract information, programs and services, publications, and products, and other sites among more.

The U.S. Education Department/OERI
gopher://gopher.ed.gov

The ED and its Office of Educational Research and Instruction offer an information server that acts as a reference desk for all things educational. Includes educational software, Goals 2000 information, and primary, secondary, and vocational information.

Voluntary National Tests—Department of Education
http://www.ed.gov/nationaltests

The President proposed in his State of the Union Address on February 4, 1997 a voluntary, annual reading test in English at grade 4 and a math test at grade 8. These tests will, for the first time in history, provide parents and teachers with information about how their students are progressing compared to other states, the nation, and other countries.

Internet Resources Relating to Education
http://www.ilt.columbia.edu/net/guides/ILTeduc.html

Columbia University's education resource list. ILT is the Institute for Learning Technologies.

State-by-State Information

American Federation of Teachers (AFT)
http://www.aft.org
http://www.aft.org//research/reports/standard/iv.htm

The American Federation of Teachers (AFT) issued *Making Standards Matter 1996 An Annual 50-State Report on Efforts to Raise Academic Standards*. Nearly every state is working to set common academic standards for their students, but the AFT report makes it clear that most states have more work to do to strengthen their standards. For example, at this time, there are only 15 states with standards in all four core categories that are clear, specific, and well-grounded in content. For a report on an individual state, go online for the AFT state-by-state analysis.

State Curriculum Frameworks and Content Standards
http://www.ed.gov/offices/OERI/statecur

Brief description of various proposed frameworks and standards projects prepared with funding from DOE and Eisenhower National Program for Math and Science Education

National Network of Regional Educational Laboratories

Appalachian Region (AEL) Specialty: Rural Education
http://www.ael.org

Western Region (WestEd) Specialty: Assessment and Accountability
http://www.fwl.org

Central Region (McREL) Specialty: Curriculum, Learning and Instruction
http://www.mcrel.org

Midwestern Region (NCREL) Specialty: Technology
http://www.ncrel.org

Northwestern Region; Specialty: School Change Processes
http://www.nwrel.org

Pacific Region; Specialty: Language and Cultural Diversity
http://prel-oahu-1.prel.hawaii.edu/

Northeastern Region; Specialty: Language and Cultural Diversity
http://www.lab.brown.edu

Mid-Atlantic Region; Specialty: Urban Education
http://www.temple.edu/departments/LSS/

Southeastern Region; Specialty: Early Childhood Education
http://www.serve.org

Southwestern Region; Specialty: Language and Cultural Diversity
http://www.sedl.org

Appendix 3

Services and
Resources

The services that follow are administered by the U.S. Department of Education to advance research, information, and communication about educational issues. Organizations should be contacted directly for more information about their research agenda and available services.

1. National Research and Development Centers

To help improve and strengthen student learning in the United States, the Office of Research supports 21 university-based national educational research and development Centers. The Centers are addressing specific topics such as early childhood education, student achievement in core academic subjects, teacher preparation and training, systemic education reform and restructuring, school governance and finance, postsecondary education, and lifelong learning. In addition, most of the Centers are also focusing on the education of disadvantaged children and youth. Many Centers are collaborating with other universities, and many work with elementary and secondary schools. All are encouraged to make sure the information they produce makes a difference and reaches parents, teachers, and others who can use it to make meaningful changes in America's schools. Some of the centers include:

National Center for Research on Educational Accountability and Teacher Evaluation
Western Michigan University
401 B. Ellsworth Hall
Kalamazoo, MI 49008
616-387-5895

National Center for Research on Cultural Diversity and Second Language Learning
University of California at Santa Cruz, Kerr Hall
Santa Cruz, CA 95064
408-459-3500

Center for Research on Effective Schooling for Disadvantaged Students
Johns Hopkins University
3505 North Charles St.
Baltimore, MD 21218
410-516-0370

National Research Center on Education in the Inner Cities
Temple University
933 Ritter Hall Annex
13th St. and Cecil B. Moore Ave.
Philadelphia, PA 19122
215-204-3001

Center for Research on Evaluation, Standards, and Student Testing (CRESST)
University of California LA
Center for the Study of Evaluation
145 Moore Hall
Los Angeles, CA 90024-1522
310-206-1532

National Research Center on the Gifted and Talented
University of Connecticut
362 Fairfield Rd. U-7
Storrs, CT 06269-2007
203-486-4826

National Center for Research in Mathematical Sciences Education
University of Wisconsin at Madison
Center for Education Research
1025 West Johnson St.
Madison, WI 53706
608-263-3605

National Center on Postsecondary Teaching, Learning, and Assessment
Pennsylvania State University
Center for the Study of Higher Education
403 S. Allen St., Ste. 104
University Park, PA 16801-5252
814-865-5917

National Center for Science Teaching and Learning
Ohio State University
1929 Kenny Rd.
Columbus, OH 43210-1015
614-292-3339

National Research Center on Student Learning
University of Pittsburgh
Learning Research and Development Center
3939 O'Hara St.
Pittsburgh, PA 15260
412-624-7457

2. ERIC Clearinghouses

Educational Resources Information Center (ERIC) is a nation-wide information network which acquires, catalogues, summarizes, and provides access to education information from all sources. ERIC produces a variety of publications and provides extensive user assistance, including AskERIC, an electronic question answering service for teachers on the Internet (askeric@ericir.syr.edu). The ERIC system includes 16 subject-specific Clearinghouses (some of which are listed below), the ERIC Processing and Reference facility.

Access ERIC maintains links to ERIC Clearinghouses and Adjunct Clearinghouses with WWW and/or Gopher sites. For more information call ACCESS ERIC at 800-538-3742.

ERIC Clearinghouse on Assessment
   and Evaluation
Catholic University of America
Department of Education
210 O'Boyle Hall
Washington, DC 20064-4035
202-319-5120

ERIC Clearinghouse on Educational
   Management
University of Oregon
1787 Agate St.
Eugene, OR 97403-5207
503-346-5043

ERIC Clearinghouse on Rural
   Education and Small Schools
1031 Quarrier St., Box 1348
Charleston, WV 25325-1348
304-347-0465

ERIC Clearinghouse on Higher
   Education
George Washington University
One Dupont Circle NW, Ste. 630
Washington, DC 20036-1183
202-296-2597

ERIC Clearinghouse on Science,
   Math & Environmental Ed.
Ohio State University
1929 Kenny Rd.
Columbus, OH 43210-1080
614-292-6717

ERIC Clearinghouse on Urban
   Education
Columbia University
Main Hall, Rm. 300
525 W. 120th St.
New York, NY 10027-9998
212-678-3433

ERIC Clearinghouse on Elementary
   and Early Childhood Education
University of Illinois
805 W. Pennsylvania Ave.
Urbana, IL 61801-4897
217-333-1386

ERIC Clearinghouse on Counseling
   and Student Services
UNC Greensboro
School of Education, Curry Bldg.
Greensboro, NC 27412-5001
919-334-4114

ERIC Clearinghouse on Disabilities
   and Gifted Education
Council for Exceptional Children
1920 Association Dr.
Reston, VA 22091-1589
703-264-9474

ERIC Clearinghouse on Information
   and Technology, Syracuse Univ.
Ctr. for Science and Technology
4th Floor, Room 194
Syracuse, NY 13244-4100
315-443-3640

3. National Center for Education Statistics Data Sets

The National Center for Education Statistics collects data on many educational areas. What follows are brief descriptions of some NCES data sets. For a complete description of all of their data sets, contact OERI at 800-424-1616 for a copy of NCES Programs and Plans.

National Assessment of Educational Progress (NAEP) provides data on the educational attainment of U.S. students. It serves as a "report card" on the national condition of education. Students are assessed at grades 4, 8, and 12 in reading and writing and subject areas that include math, science, U.S. history, and world geography. Contact: Education Assessment Division, 202-219-1761.

Common Core of Data (CCD) is a comprehensive, annual, national statistical database of all public elementary and secondary schools and school districts, which contains data that are comparable across all states. Contact: Elementary and Secondary Education Statistics Division, 202-219-1335.

National Education Longitudinal Study of 1988 (NELS:88) follows children starting at 8th grade and will update information throughout the 1990s. NELS:88 is designed to provide trend data about critical transitions experienced by young people as they develop, attend school, and embark on their careers. Contact: Elementary and Secondary Education Statistics Division, 202-219-1777.

4. National Information Center for Children and Youth with Disabilities (NICHCY)

NICHCY provides information and technical assistance free of charge to families, professionals, caregivers, advocates, agencies, and others in helping children and youth with disabilities to become participating members of the community. NICHCY offers databases, publications and newsletters, updated fact sheets, briefing papers, and parents' guides. Contact: NICHCY/Suzanne Ripley, P.O. Box 1492, Washington, DC 20013, 800-695-0285.

Appendix 4

More High-Frequency Words

The Second 100

get	through	back	much	go	good	new
write	our	me	man	too	any	day
same	between	right	look	think	around	also
another	came	come	work	three	must	here
because	does	part	even	place	well	such
take	why	help	put	different	away	again
off	went	old	number	great	tell	men
say	small	every	found	still	name	should
home	big	give	air	line	set	own
under	read	last	never	us	left	end
along	while	might	next	sound	below	saw
something	thought	both	few	those	always	show
large	often	together	asked	house	don't	world
going	want	school	until	important	form	food
keep	children					

The Third 100

feet	land	side	without	boy	once	kind
animals	life	enough	took	four	head	above
began	almost	live	page	got	earth	need

far	hand	high	year	mother	light	country
father	let	night	picture	being	study	second
soon	story	since	white	ever	paper	hard
near	sentence	better	best	across	during	today
however	sure	knew	it's	try	told	young
sun	thing	whole	hear	example	heard	several
change	answer	room	sea	against	top	turned
learn	point	city	play	toward	five	himself
usually	money	seen	didn't	morning	car	I'm
body	upon	family	later	turn	move	face
door	cut	done	group	true	half	red
fish	plants					

The Fourth 100

living	black	eat	short	United	run	book
gave	order	open	ground	cold	really	table
remember	tree	course	front	American	space	inside
ago	sad	early	I'll	learned	brought	close
nothing	though	idea	before	lived	became	add
become	grow	draw	yet	less	wind	behind
cannot	letter	among	able	dog	shown	mean
English	rest	perhaps	certain	six	feel	fire
ready	green	yes	built	special	ran	full
town	complete	oh	person	anything	hot	hold
state	list	stood	hundred	ten	fast	felt
kept	notice	can't	strong	voice	probably	area
horse	matter	stand	box	start	that's	class
piece	surface	river	common	stop	am	talk
whether	fine					

The Fifth 100

round	dark	past	ball	girl	road	blue
instead	either	held	already	warm	gone	finally
summer	understand	moon	animal	mind	outside	power
problem	longer	winter	deep	heavy	carefully	follow
beautiful	everyone	leave	game	system	bring	watch
shall	dry	fact	within	floor	ice	ship
themselves	begin	third	quite	everything	carry	sat
distance	although	possible	heart	real	simple	snow
rain	suddenly	leaves	easy	lay	size	wild
weather	miss	pattern	sky	waked	main	center
someone	field	stay	itself	boat	question	wide
least	tiny	hour	happened	foot	care	low
else	gold	build	glass	rock	tall	alone
bottom	walk	check	fall	poor	map	friend
language	job					

Index